Spreading Rebellion

Spanish Maritime Radicalism in the Americas, 1875–1930

Bieito Alonso and David M. Struthers

AK
PRESS

© 2025 Bieito Alonso and David M. Struthers
This edition © 2025 AK Press

ISBN 978-1-84935-623-7
E-ISBN: 978-1-84935-624-4
LCCN: 2025937206

AK Press   AK Press
370 Ryan Avenue #100   33 Tower Street
Chico, CA 95973   Edinburgh, EH6, 7BN
USA   Scotland
www.akpress.org   www.akuk.com
akpress@akpress.org   akuk@akpress.org

Please contact us to request the latest AK Press distribution catalog,
which features books, pamphlets, zines, and stylish apparel published
and/or distributed by AK Press. Alternatively, visit our websites for the
complete catalog, latest news, and secure ordering.

Cover illustration by Agustín Comotto
Printed in the United States of America on acid-free paper

To Sara, for everything
—Bieito Alonso

To my parents, Sue and David, for their lifelong support and my daughter, Freya, for her hope and inspiration
—David M. Struthers

If there were no sailors and firemen, the ship would not move. If the workers don't work, not a penny goes into the rich pockets. The boat was bought and prepared with money obtained by squeezing the blood of other workers. It's money they stole from us. The rich and we are like parents and children.

—**Kobayashi Takiji**, *Kanikōsen*

Contents

Introduction

This book is not intended to be, nor can it be, a comprehensive history of Spanish sailors across the expanses of the Atlantic Ocean. Rather, it documents the activities of an almost entirely male migrant labor force that left Spain without families, often at a young age, to seek work on ships and ports across the Americas between 1875 and 1930. These workers contributed to the development and consolidation of maritime unionism. Inspired by Peter Linebaugh and Marcus Rediker's work on eighteenth-century working-class radicalism, our goal is to recover the lost history of the multiethnic working class essential to the expansion of capitalism and the development of the modern global economy.[1] Reclaiming their histories as multidirectional migrants throughout the Americas is essential because this is how they understood themselves in their occupations and class. Spanish sailors and other maritime workers built organizations to defend their aspirations and desires where they lived and where they worked. Indeed, Spanish migrants to the Americas did so much more effectively and with better forethought than their counterparts in Spain laboring in the maritime industry during the same period.

Investigating the trajectories of these migrant workers necessitates understanding their lives within the broader processes that worked to obscure working-class voices. The direct forms of repression governments and businesses unleashed against them combined with their marginalized position in global capitalism to constrain their historical record. Haitian-American anthropologist Michel-Rolph Trouillot traced the historical process of "silencing the past" through source creation, archiving, retrieval, and interpretation.[2] Marginalized people created fewer sources. Archives of the period, often state-run, were run by people who rarely saw the records working-class people managed to create as worthy of preservation. Generations of historians did not see value in retrieving the sources available, nor did they value the migrant laborers' voices while interpreting the past.[3] As we grapple with these factors in our research, we also must recognize how archivists' and historians' continued power to silence working-class voices is supported by the ability of states to hold history captive through the power to define what lies within their boundaries and obscure what lies beyond. This makes it more difficult to analyze any spatial sphere that undermines or questions the supposed universality of states: the spaces in between.[4]

The space examined in this book is central to our contribution. The idea of the Atlantic as a binding geographical element to synthesize cultural identity throughout the Atlantic territories has received little attention in Spanish historiography.[5] Yet Spanish migration to the Americas is an essential element in contemporary Spanish historiography in which the Atlantic emerges as an indirect protagonist in this diaspora. The ocean functioned as a natural support channeling humans between entry and exit points where freight and lives joined. However, Spanish historians rarely present the Atlantic as an autonomous space giving meaning to what it integrated.[6]

More broadly, Atlantic history was an intermittent subject and undervalued as an object of study until the end of the twentieth century. The works of historians Linebaugh and Rediker stand out in interpreting the Atlantic world as a framework of transnational relations by describing the historical connections binding Atlantic ports in the seventeenth and eighteenth centuries. They document the lives of people struggling through various states of freedom—proletarianized workers, indentured people, prisoners, and enslaved people—and forging connections through dramatic forms of resistance in workshops, public space, prisons, barracks, ships, and plantations. Sailors, dockworkers, laborers with various skills, sex workers, and pirates forged new ideas of freedom and equality in these sites and through their struggles to live life on their own terms.[7]

David Armitage defines the space of these events as "circum-Atlantic history" and views the base unit of Atlantic history as the ocean itself before human protagonists intervened.[8] Oceans are natural bodies, after all, one of the few historical categories with a non-artificial geography, in contrast to the shifting and imperfect conjunctions of political loyalties and state boundaries. Even so, some researchers identify the Cold War roots of the development of Atlantic history with an ideological objective of uniting the history of "Western Europe" with the rise of US hegemonic power.[9] In this sense, the Atlantic as such was a European invention, a consequence of successive waves of navigation, exploration, colonization, administration, and imagination. It was a European invention not because the Europeans were its only inhabitants but because they first connected the four shores of Europe, Africa, North America, and South America into a single entity, both as a transportation network and as a representation of a specific geographic reality.[10] The precise boundaries of that ocean were, of course, fluid. It is less clear where it ended than what territories it connected since Europeans thought of the ocean as a single body of water in motion and not as the sum of the Earth's seven seas.

The space of Atlantic history, then, is an identifiable area of exchange, circulation, and transmission. It includes the

Atlantic shores of continents and islands but only to the extent
that they are part of an oceanic history and not a set of national
or regional histories bordering the Atlantic. Our interest is to
capture stories of people that crossed the ocean—often repeat-
edly—lived on its shores, and participated in the communities
they helped build economically, socially, and ideologically. This
is a particularly cohesive concept because it insists on the fundamental importance that diaspora stories—which included
stories of mass genocides—had in Africa and the Americas in
the creation of the culture of modernity.[11]

The history uncovered in this book is circum-Atlantic in
two ways: it incorporates the entire Atlantic basin, and it traces
continued circulations throughout the Atlantic world. It is,
above all, a transnational history that moves away from statist
delimitation. However, to claim the transnational is not only
to affirm that historical processes develop in different places
but also, as Isabel Hofmeyr suggests, that such processes are
built into the movement between different places, spaces, and
regions. Therefore, the significance of a transnational study is
"its fundamental concern with movements, flows and circulation, not simply as a theme or motive but as an analytical set
of methods that defines the enterprise itself."[12] Those historical
processes, include, for instance, migration, trade flows, and
technology transfer.

We are then faced with a perspective that proposes a recon-
sideration of how to understand geographical spaces and joins
with a more recent historiography that allows us to rethink the
ways subversive cultures circulate, mutate, and are reinvented
over time.[13] In doing so, it is important to not allow a transnational approach to eliminate locally grounded perspectives and
processes. Rather, Lourenzo Fernández Prieto reminds us that
transnational history "must be compatible with the naturaliza-
tion of local history, but it must recover from the local level the
old ideal of universal history to build global explanations, thus
overcoming the confrontation, today unnecessary, between

4

universal and local."[14] Finally, this local history responds to social and political demands that are expressed in the most intimate of spheres, and this location allows the returning of silenced histories to the public stage.

Documenting the local and national contexts of Buenos Aires, Havana, and New York is essential to weaving together the network that linked maritime workers in the western Atlantic. Explaining similarities and differences is an essential task toward integrating these workers into a common map and providing context to their shared experiences. Local space should be made explicit, but docks, newspapers, cafés, and even boats themselves must also be protagonists in this story.

A global economic framework

Global production and trade increased between 1870 and 1914, with major powers seeing growth rates of both trade and gross domestic product (GDP) exceeding 35 percent. Capital and goods moved quickly and relatively freely across national and imperial borders. European technology, military power, and commercial interests combined into distinct imperial projects that divided the world among a few large states as World War I erupted in 1914. The British Empire, for example, already occupied a quarter of the land of the Earth with a population of eight hundred million people in 1900.[15] Jack London witnessed these globalizing processes and expressed his amazement at the extraordinary shrinking of the planet, through which "the East was made next-door neighbor to the West."[16]

Globalizing processes have deep historical roots. Indeed, the gradual integration of globalized production and consumption goes back many centuries, marked by periods of ascendance and retrenchment, but the confluence of institutional and technological change after the Napoleonic Wars (1803–15) increased their pace. European states began accepting the presence of foreign flags in maritime trade, but they initially maintained discriminatory surcharges or tariffs to favor their national fleets. England, which became the world's leading transporter of goods in this period, unilaterally eliminated navigation laws in 1849, thereby opening its ports to foreign shipping fleets. Scandinavia and the Netherlands followed before Germany, France, Spain, and Italy made similar changes. The Paris Declaration of 1856, which struck a blow against privateering and piracy on the high seas, and the rescinding of laws restricting competition in international maritime navigation ushered in a period of free trade and turned maritime transport into an international business.

International relations and trade agreements also shifted during the second half of the nineteenth century. The British initiated a process of trade liberalization by abolishing grain and shipping laws. The UK and France signed a treaty in 1860 that further opened trade. Bilateral trade agreements, increasingly common, enabled growth in international trade.[17] Yet trade liberalization fell in and out of favor depending on the political and economic winds, and the 1870s saw a return to protectionism.

Continued improvements to transportation and communication technology facilitated this period of globalization through changes in trade policy and national politics. They increased the efficiency of shipping goods and integrated geographically distant places. Market integration, measured by the convergence of prices between countries, defined this era's economic transformation. Never before had such a convergence of international prices occurred, despite increases in world trade since the sixteenth century.[18] International trade increased dramatically, and capital moved, as did workers through migration. After 1870, these connected processes made possible the integration of continental and transoceanic markets, an international division of labor, and the convergence of the leading global economies.[19]

6

The rise of steamers

Maritime transport also changed significantly in the second half of the nineteenth century as the prevalence of steamships increased in transatlantic travel and cargo shipping after 1865. Steamers had clear benefits over sailing ships. Passengers and merchants desired reliable transit times without delays caused by variable wind speeds, and they were willing to pay higher prices for this convenience. Despite these obvious advantages, steam took some time to prevail over sails in maritime transport, and competition between clippers and steamships initially kept prices in check.

Steamers came to monopolize maritime transport for two fundamental reasons. First, the opening of the Suez Canal in 1869 shortened the route between Europe and Asia by shifting transit to inland seas with less wind than the open oceans. Second, technical innovations favored steamships. Iron (1860) and then steel (1879) replaced wooden hulls and made possible the casting of large propeller blades. The development of compound steam engines, with double (1869) and triple expansion furnaces (1874), increased the efficiency of steam power. This reduced the volume of coal storage space required, which increased space for passengers and goods. Large increases in public investment to expand and improve ports supported these remarkable changes in maritime shipping. Around 1880, the efficiency gains of maritime machines reduced crew and navigation costs and made it possible to remove auxiliary sails from steamships. Steamships eventually reduced ocean freight rates in the Atlantic by 45 percent and definitively prevailed in long-distance maritime transport by the turn of the twentieth century.[20] The United Kingdom maintained leadership in global maritime transport and shipbuilding in this period despite growth in these industries in the United States, Japan, and Italy.

The process of replacing wind propulsion with steam engines radically altered crew composition, size, and the organization of work onboard ships. Maritime historian Enric García has explained the multiple changes that accompanied the incorporation of mechanical propulsion. New sailors did not share the traditional ethos of those sailing wind-driven vessels rooted in relationships among sailors with diverse skills. Task fragmentation increased, which weakened worker control over some labor processes. On sailboats, all crew members commonly gained skills sufficient to help with tasks outside of their specialty. On steamers, mechanization segmented tasks and increased the technical knowledge required, which constrained workers to their roles. On board, the division of labor increased between supervisors (officers) and crew.[21] Historian Eric Sager writes that the increasing complexity of steamships compartmentalized knowledge, which worked to increase the separation between officers and manual laborers on vessels.[22] The spatial organization of steamships below deck, now separated into watertight compartments, and fragmented job categories broke the traditional bonds of crews.

The new occupations of machinists, firemen, and shovelers fitted into shipboard hierarchies with officers supervising subordinates, replacing crew trimming sails on deck as the key element in ship propulsion. This transformation shifted seafaring labor from something resembling an artisanal craft to mechanized tasks that diminished the need for traditional skills for most crew. The increased size of steamers also increased the number of crew required in new roles. Sailors accounted for approximately three-quarters of crew members on clippers, but topside crew did not exceed one-quarter of personnel on steamers, and 45 percent of crew worked deep below deck in the engine room.[23]

During the rise of steamers, large shipping companies suffered serious losses between 1892 and 1894 because excess capacity drove prices down. Shippers responded through cost reduction measures. The newer and larger ships could still generate profits owing to their increased efficiency over older,

smaller vessels. In 1894 and 1895, all the large shipping companies definitively transitioned to large steamers, and the industry
consolidated. A new economic crisis in 1901 further contributed
to business concentration. For example, the tonnage handled by
eight of Spain's largest shipping companies reached 45 percent
in 1915, while the eight largest shippers in the United Kingdom
carried 42 percent of the freight in 1918 and 1919.[24]

All seafarers saw their prior strength diminished in the face
of these changes. Stronger companies even diminished the ability of captains to directly manage the ships they commanded.[25]
Historian Juan Zamora Terrés argues that the second half of
the nineteenth century saw the total transformation of navigation and nautical sciences, the economy of trade by sea, the
makeup of maritime companies, the techniques and economy
of shipbuilding, and labor relations both on board and more
broadly in the industry, and this, he says, profoundly changed
the mentality of seamen.[26]

These globalizing forces also facilitated the rise of new migratory processes, in which maritime workers themselves participated, especially drawing Europeans to work in North America.
This was the context in which migrant maritime workers from
Spain sailed the Atlantic and docked in ports throughout North
and South America, joining labor organizations that spread as
they traveled.

Firemen, sailors, and working conditions

Sailors have always been indispensable on ships, although
changing technology shifted the character of their labor over
time. The arrival of steamships in the nineteenth century
changed the types of labor and the spatial arrangement of
work. Steamers ushered in the loss of professional identity that
impacted every occupation on board, from officers to cooks,
but it had a special meaning for sailors through obsolescence

and proletarianization. Rather than workers trimming sails on deck, steamships required engineers, firemen, and shovelers below deck in the engine room. Perception of these changes among crew helped bring to sea the concept widely used on land: the proletariat.

Rediker argues that the proletarianization process in the merchant navy arrived before the technological transition to steamers. A complex division of labor, coordinated and synchronized work rhythms, and shift work, all closely supervised and enforced by a strict surveillance and disciplinary system, increasingly typified shipboard work. Alienation came to be expressed by referring to workers as "hands."[27] Pushing back, lower deck workers acted with sailors to define themselves in their organizations as "workers of the sea." This was a new industrial expression that broke with deeply rooted traditions of class, status, and position.[28]

Socio-economic questions undoubtedly played an important role in building a new community; the organization of labor on steamships also influenced this cultural expression of sailors' economic position. Steamship workers identified with the industrial world as ships now relied on machines, pipes, measuring devices, fire, and coal, as well as through the dictatorship of schedules and the scarcity of private space. Bruce Nelson finds that as their size increased, ships became large floating factories similar to their landside counterparts, with space segmented into different levels and sections. Bridges, decks, mezzanines, warehouses, engine rooms, coal pits, kitchens, toilets, and lockers created a complex geography that favored crew segmentation and broke the traditional bow-stern coordinates of smaller ships by extending the vertical axis.[29] Changes in living and working environments included larger crews with weaker social bonds. Steamers also marked the loss of traditional values of the sea shared by sailors and influenced changes in the perception of work and its role on board. In this sense, the transition from sail to steam power at sea is comparable to small workshops becoming large factories on land.

Moreover, steamers had complex physical environments, with difficult access between decks through dark mazes of stairs.[30] Steamers reduced crew spaces in favor of increasing cargo holds or passenger capacity, relegating crews to narrow, dirty, poorly ventilated cabins, far below deck, often next to hazardous material storage and latrines where noxious gases, odors, and steam polluted the air. Conditions on board most vessels were truly inhumane.

Many official reports documented spatial limitations on ships. For instance, a medical officer at the Port of London expressed alarm that cattle stables were wider than sailors' cabins. A US Navy surgeon stressed, "Sailors suffered, on a recurrent basis, diseases, almost all of them caused by the polluted atmosphere and by the unhealthy conditions in which they ate and slept." A British officer warned that conditions on the ship *Comfort* were worse than those of a prison, with the added risk of drowning.[31] Crews sailing on all seas knew: "Cabins are too wide for a coffin and too narrow for a tomb."[32]

Shipping companies filled their need for labor in the new job categories in the engine room and staffing passenger vessels through a pool of transnational and immigrant workers. By the end of the nineteenth century, immigrant workers dominated in most of the powerful merchant navies. In the Americas, nine out of ten sailors were foreign-born at that time.[33] The reasons for hiring immigrant sailors were not exclusively demographic. For many workers seeking employment, the extreme harshness of life at sea limited the appeal of crew work. Most preferred working on land, even at a lower salary, if they had the option. Migrants without credentialed skills who had fewer opportunities to work on the docks or elsewhere landside met the need for onboard labor.[34]

The arrival of such a large number of immigrants from diverse cultural and linguistic backgrounds created friction on board. Spanish-speaking sailors encountered fewer difficulties working with Spanish-speaking officers and foremen than with supervisors with whom they did not share a common language. In Argentina and Cuba, officers and crew spoke Spanish, which limited communication problems in the management of daily life on board steamers and on the docks. A common language eased relationships between new migrants and established communities in these two locations. In the United States, the situation was very different. Few Spanish maritime workers spoke even rudimentary English, and they did not prioritize learning it because of their extraordinary mobility and because they did not view their stay as permanent. Labor disputes arising from language misunderstandings recurred—with punishment commonplace—on ships with English-speaking officers and Spanish-speaking crew.

Communication difficulties occurred up and down the management structure but also horizontally between fellow migrants. Language was at the heart of maritime organizational models in the Americas. Spaniards joined craft societies or maritime federations without apparent difficulty in Spanish-speaking countries. In the United States, Spanish workers opted to develop "ethnic" unions, exemplified by the Unión de Fogoneros, Cabos y Engrasadores del Atlántico (Marine Firemen's, Watertenders', and Oilers' Union of the Atlantic). The union affiliated with larger white and English-dominated unions, but they maintained organizational autonomy. Spanish union leaders associated with Latin American, Portuguese, and Italian workers, but they were reluctant and even hostile to the idea of collaborating with organizations dominated by Anglos or northern Europeans.[35]

Coexistence on board through shared working and living conditions also contributed to community, solidarity, and fellowship among crew within segmented job roles. Outside of their working hours, crew members spent their free time together in their own spaces, however limited. They found time for conversation, play, and camaraderie exclusively among crewmates. The bonds between workers arose from the very conditions and relations of their work, in particular the need to navigate in a fragile and isolated ship, surrounded by dangers of the sea and the furnaces on board. There were other dangers, no less serious, stemming from the officers and the firms employing everyone on board.

There was an unreconcilable conflict between the needs and imperatives of a globalized capitalist economy and a transnational moral economy of seafarers, what we might call a collectivism of necessity. Seafarers resorted to a complex process of negotiation and resistance to increase their rights and advantages and to defend and protect themselves from accidents, disease, and abusive treatment. Maritime labor consciousness transformed into a class consciousness as seafarers developed broader patterns of association, affinity, and identification. The process was visible both on land and on the sea in acts of collective resistance. Sailors used their mobility to improve their lives, create ties with other workers, and form a new kind of mobile community. These mobile workers occupied a strategic position in the division of labor that put them into contact with many other workers with whom they exchanged experiences and information.[36]

Shared experiences brought widespread benefits. This led to the creation of unions of seafarers and dockworkers, aggressive campaigns for legislative reforms, and fights for workplace control. Traditional forms of brutal discipline on ships also became less oppressive. Complaints continued over physical abuse, but the demands of maritime workers mostly shifted to wages, like many millions of other workers, but above all regarded living conditions on board and job degradation on land.[37] In Argentina, sailors complained, "Who does not know, in fact, the dirty pigsty of some boats, whether they are called cabins or ranches, where we are often forced to spend part of our existence, with the very serious danger of contracting a serious disease? It is not possible to continue to contemplate that a large number of our brothers rot in dirty rooms, without any ventilation, plagued by disgusting bugs, rooms that become more odious and stinky [in] warm climates. . . . There are ships that look like vultures, and from them come the crewmen like lizards from their caves."[38] In the United States, criticism of the racism impacting labor relations on ships shaped grievances.[39] Many US whites viewed Spain as an enemy during and after the Spanish-American War, and negative views toward Spaniards often took racial forms. Racism also had a transnational perspective as Spaniards spread throughout the continent, intertwined with the exploitation that characterized the maritime sector.

A determined community

The harsh working conditions encountered by Spanish maritime workers in the Atlantic acted as a fermenting agent for labor organizing. The intricacies of how they transformed workplace grievances into militant labor organizing, how they translated their desires into a language of protest, and how they created a wide-ranging ideological movement that communicated across the Atlantic is the story that unfolds in the following chapters. Yet labor exploitation alone does not explain the very human and social processes of organization. In some cases in the United States, the marginalization of workers along ethnic and racial lines and the activation of a long catalog of prejudice against migrants who did not speak English played a crucial role in the formation of maritime unionism among Spanish firemen and their strong radical currents. These factors also brought Spanish firemen closer to Italians, Portuguese, and Greeks in labor conflicts and unions as they shared similar experiences of exclusion and mistreatment.

Similar to the process that Winston James documented among Caribbean migrants, social thought among Spanish sailors arose from transnational interactions and connections. James described Black contact zones as intermediate spaces of negotiation between cultures, American imperial enclaves where Caribbean migrant workers exchanged experiences and ideas to form common ideological ground.[40] For James, the main contact points were located in the Panama Canal Zone, through which 150,000 workers from the Caribbean migrated in the early twentieth century, in fruit plantations owned by US corporations throughout Central America, and in the sugarcane plantations of the Dominican Republic and Cuba, with hundreds of thousands of workers from Jamaica, Haiti, and the Leeward Islands. Many Caribbeans also migrated to work in the oil industry in Curaçao, Aruba, and Venezuela.[41] Previous political and union experience, in addition to their extensive travel, favored Caribbean radicalization before their eventual arrival in the United States. Many Caribbeans developed an internationalist, pan-African perspective through their interaction with Black people in other countries and through their observations of a common oppression suffered by Black communities around the world.[42]

In the case of the Spanish seafaring community based in New York City, it does not seem so obvious that the existence of these contact zones generated a radical social consciousness. Some of the Spanish seamen briefly stayed in Cuba or Puerto Rico, working as sailors or firemen, before their arrival in the United States. Others, not in large numbers, had worked in the Panama Canal Zone and integrated, like the Caribbeans, into its segmented occupational statuses. Most came directly from Spain, primarily from Galicia. From the late nineteenth century on, they based their decisions to migrate to the United States on information they obtained from those settled in the Atlantic harbors, with the hope of obtaining better wages and working conditions than in Spain. Leading organizers of Spanish maritime workers were all agitators who regularly moved between Caribbean ports, and they ideologically developed in close contact with the anarchist communities in these places. They were mostly anarcho-syndicalists in ideological orientation.

Setting aside those with a preformed radical consciousness, in what sense did the contact zones influence the gestation of advanced social thought? In the United States, the marginalization, exploitation, and degradation faced by these migrant workers increased their radicalization. In this regard, the contact locations were for sailors or fireman as mobile as their own lives, changing and flexible. Among Spanish maritime workers, another factor facilitated their internal cohesion as a group with defined interests: the rejection of the Spanish migrant elite, composed mostly of professionals, journalists, merchants, and industrialists who sought integration and recognition in societies throughout the Americas. Unlike the protection exercised in the United States—for instance, by the British Crown over its Caribbean subjects—Spanish consular authorities incessantly criticized the Spanish-language labor press, particularly syndicalist newspapers such as *Cultura Obrera*, and by extension all organizers and anarchists, with labels as blunt as "scum that [have] dishonored the Spanish community."[43]

There was also a strong personal factor. Migrants in these locations encountered the most active ideological currents, whether anarchist, socialist, or reformist, and workers identified proponents of these positions as moral references. The same people who erected social centers and contributed to newspapers from *Cultura Obrera* in Brooklyn to *La Voz del Marino* in Buenos Aires sowed the seeds planted in resistance societies and in industrial unions. Nothing can be explained without the dedication of organizers such as Juan Martínez de la Graña, Genaro Pazos, Constante Carballo, Juan Arévalo, Manuel Rey, and Pedro Esteve.

The power exercised by seafarers through their mobility also helped stimulate the process of organizing maritime workers on land. As Peter Cole writes, dockworkers have power.[44] Dockworkers have a power integral to the development of maritime transport, the world's first global industry, and they were instrumental in capitalism's rise. Their vital position contributed to the power of so-called unskilled workers, power accumulated through collective action, ideological commitment, and sheer willpower. Similar to people in other circumstances, they used their influence to improve their destiny. Although often ignored by elites, maritime workers, whether in port or at sea, were essential to the cities which they were linked. Alice Mah writes that these workers are the iconic symbols of urban identity in port towns, and in many ways the history of dockworkers represents identities and mythologies that are the backbone of historic ports.[45]

Investigating maritime labor history necessitates developing an understanding of how port workers and sailors struggled for the power to disrupt trade and the economy itself—locally, nationally, and globally. Atlantic port cities in the Americas had different trade connections, histories of work and hiring practices, and migrant communities. They present a rich human and urban context to examine new and old global connections and provide a window to understand how port workers built an occupational subculture in which they used their strategic position in capitalism's supply chain to improve their own conditions and contribute to far-reaching social movements.

We close the Atlantic circle by returning to immigration. The protagonists of this book are migrants linked to maritime work. Many of them labored in jobs connected to maritime trade in Spain before their initial migration. They were sailors, firemen, oilers, or fishermen who left to improve their economic conditions. Most were from coastal areas of Spain, especially Galicia. Migrants originally from Spain's interior provinces lacked experience and skills for shipboard work; they sought maritime work as a temporary solution to poor prospects at home. Some Spanish migrants were "mobile agitators" who moved through the countries on the Atlantic coast of the Americas to build an internationalist movement with broad, often universalist aspirations. Organizers such as Juan Martínez de la Graña or Constante Carballo articulated the position of multinational workers of the sea and created a network led by stevedores and firemen that collided with businesses and states up and down the Atlantic coast.

There were also clearly differentiated tendencies in this milieu. For example, Juan Arévalo organized in a Cuban movement tinged by reformism and a vague pan-Americanism. This movement maintained an effective presence in the political life of Cuba in the style of a trade union lobby that negotiated with the governments holding office and guaranteed itself institutional power. This model contrasts with the radical and libertarian project of anarchists and syndicalists, which predominated among Spanish maritime workers based in South America and the United States. The Atlantic world in the late-nineteenth century and early-twentieth centuries was a space of hope and contradiction, a world unto itself that still helps us understand who we were and were we might want to go.

CHAPTER ONE

Life on the Docks

Libertarians and Trade Unionists in Buenos Aires

The export of agricultural goods constituted the core of
Argentina's economy in the late-nineteenth and early-twentieth
centuries. Maritime transport brought these products to global
markets. Steamers of varied draft cruised up the coastal rivers
or along the Patagonian coast, consolidating goods at the Port
of Buenos Aires before their international export. The central-
ity of river and maritime transport in Argentina's agricultural
export economy increased the potential organizing strength
of workers in this sector. Sailors and port workers labored in
essential occupations and could maximize the potential of job
actions along key chokepoints to strike blows deep into the
heart of the country's economy. Maritime workers recognized
the strength of their economic position and their potential
power if organized through unions and other outlets for collective struggle. Shipping companies too concentrated power
commensurate to their economic position, and the government often intervened on their behalf. The combination of
these forces gave labor conflicts at ports particular visibility
and intensity. Between 1885 and 1905, anarchist militants and
socialists channeled maritime labor struggles through resistance societies. After 1905, a new form of revolutionary syndicalism elevated the role of direct action in constructing a new

society through class struggle rather than via unions focused on immediate material gains for workers. This outlook rejected most political means of struggle to create a society based on associations of workers.[1]

Reorganizing Argentina's economy, politics, port cities, and labor

Argentina's economy expanded from the middle of the nineteenth century until World War I interrupted global trade. The period between 1880 and World War I brought the highest economic growth in the country's history, and the economy expanded again during the 1920s before the global economic depression of the 1930s. The expansion of agricultural and livestock production joined with human population increases to feed growth by consolidating a national market and generating exports. The total volume of exports grew sixteen-fold between 1870 and 1929, as the GDP increased at a rate of 6 percent per year. Argentina fundamentally changed over the second half of the nineteenth century by reorienting and expanding its agricultural production to the export market, an outward growth model that rearticulated political and economic relationships and rapidly expanded cities connected to trade.[2]

The economic transition consolidated through the closing decades of the nineteenth century as workers constructed the transportation infrastructure necessary to support increased trade. Many thousands of workers built ocean and river transport works and railroad lines to facilitate capitalist development. In 1878, the only Argentine port capable of receiving large ships was immediately south of Buenos Aires at Boca de Riachuelo. Deep draft ocean vessels like ocean liners and cargo ships had to anchor in the outer harbor of Buenos Aires. Port workers would then complete the labor-intensive and time-consuming process of transferring passengers and cargo to smaller vessels before finally offloading to customs and administrative buildings. Between 1890 and 1897, the Madero Project expanded the Port of Buenos Aires with new docks, canals, and dikes to improve efficiency, which further solidified the dominant role of the capital city. In addition to long-distance open-ocean shipping, thousands of smaller vessels traveled along the rivers and coasts of Argentina and to the neighboring countries of Uruguay, Brazil, and Paraguay. Global maritime shipping required the integration of supporting vessels to link global transportation networks.[3]

Argentina joined an increasingly integrated world market as an exporter of agricultural products, which reshaped its rural economic and social structure. The construction of railroads and advances in refrigerated shipping enabled the expansion of cattle production, instead of sheep rearing, farther into the hinterlands, including Patagonia. The consolidation of wealth and land ownership increased, notably from the 1910s. Large often-absentee landowners expanded their holdings as peasants, sharecroppers, and harvest workers provided the labor. At the beginning of the 1910s, a succession of agrarian conflicts occurred, driven by the demands of *chacareros* (sharecroppers) and rural laborers for longer and more affordable leases and freedom to market the goods they harvested and improve their living conditions.[4]

Economic expansion also reshaped urban life. The population of Argentina's three major port cities—Buenos Aires, Rosario, and Bahía Blanca—increased rapidly because of these economic shifts. Major urban development projects accompanying port construction remade these cities. The scale of change was immense. Before 1880, the Argentine industrial sector consisted of workshops based on manual labor with little or no mechanization; there were no large modern factories. Most of the workshops processed raw materials extracted in the countryside such as leather and wood. There was a small textile industry, and the metallurgical industry consisted of small workshops of blacksmiths and boilermakers. In 1880, work in Argentine cities still occurred in small workshops, often organized through family relationships. By 1910, the manufacturing sector made up only 15 percent of gross domestic product, but the vast scale of expansion of the agricultural sector obscured significant manufacturing growth.[5]

Predominantly debt-financed public spending on infrastructure, railways, ports, schools, and urban development projects remade urban areas. Retail trade in cities expanded, and many workers found employment in the sector. Wholesale trade traditionally related to imports began to shift with the growth of local production. Some wholesalers diversified their businesses with both imported and domestic products, and new import companies emerged specializing in selling goods to inland markets. These firms generally headquartered in Buenos Aires, Rosario, or even a smaller city such as Bahía Blanca, with branch offices in the provinces through which they managed their interior trade. The urban economy during this period included industrial workers, domestic workers, commerce, construction trades, dockworkers, and transportation workers.[6]

The export and import of goods and large-scale immigration created a feverish and intense rhythm at ports. Laura Caruso documented the process of Argentine port areas becoming economic, social, political and cultural cores. They were areas in which diverse types of work and cultural exchanges occurred, contained several market plazas, in addition to places for leisure, trade, and political organizing.[7] Ports played a crucial role in the country's urban life and focused the tensions and conflicts of urban growth and economic change over matters such as wages and industrial organization. This was particularly true for the country's largest city and port, Buenos Aires. The port concentrated the largest amount of labor in Argentina and all of Latin America at the end of the nineteenth century. In 1895, approximately eleven thousand people worked in the merchant marine, half of whom embarked from the Port of Buenos Aires.

By 1905, approximately twenty thousand dockworkers labored at the ports of Buenos Aires, Rosario, and Bahía Blanca.[8] At the centenary of Argentina's independence in 1910, the Port of Buenos Aires was the eighth-largest in the world in terms of total value.[9]

The industries and economic activities concentrated at or near the port connected local, regional, and global economies. Workers labored in various jobs linked to exports: maritime tradesmen, longshore workers, stevedores, shipbuilders, and *carreros* (cart drivers), in addition to merchants and tradesmen in the workshops adjacent to the port. Wholesaling goods was the most important economic activity at the port, and workers transported goods through warehouses, cereal silos, and refrigerated storage areas. Small-scale commerce in shops, coffeehouses, and inns also flourished, supporting both customers (through their services) and their proprietors. Skilled workers built and repaired vessels in the shipyard, and the naval equipment industry rounded out the port economy. Beyond laboring in or near the port, workers made the port and its surroundings their family and social environment through their homes, recreation, union halls, and meeting spaces.[10] The importance of the port in Argentine life is difficult to overstate. It played an outsized role in the political, economic, and social life of the entire country. Its influence was so powerful that the residents of Buenos Aires are known as Porteñas and Porteños.

In 1904, sixty thousand people lived in the port neighborhood of Buenos Aires. Italian immigrant families predominated, and the area was a "true Babel," with Slovenians (many having migrated to Argentina with Italian passports), Spaniards from different regions, Greeks, and Turks. These residents formed a diverse group that impacted the material and social transformation of the port and the city through their work. Residents formed community through traditions and experiences that they melded into a shared culture that shaped the forms and times of protest, popular festivals, and the everyday environment. Community formation and the development of radical ideas were inseparable.[11]

Almost exclusively men labored as dockworkers and sailors in this time and place. Dangerous, grueling, and precarious work performed outdoors through all seasons made their lives difficult. Frequent accidents and long working hours, inclement weather, and the excessive weight of the bags and bales workers carried broke down bodies.[12] A strong seasonal rhythm linked to the agricultural cycle, one shared with wide sectors of the labor market of the time, characterized work at the port. The harvest season during southern summer, between December and March, brought the highest level of port activity, with the loading of goods destined for international markets. The demand for labor peaked in these months, especially for unskilled laborers, making this a propitious moment for job actions. Most of the strikes declared by maritime and port workers took place between December and February.[13]

Employers drew from an abundant reserve labor force and leveraged their power to keep salaries and professional status low for maritime workers, a situation comparable to many European and North American ports during this period.[14] Onshore and onboard ships, thousands of workers shared common experiences as they carried out their daily tasks, which they cultivated into extensive social and cultural networks through their organizing and personal connections. These networks contributed to their militancy and organizing strength. The strategic position of dockworkers and other maritime workers at chokepoints of global capitalism concentrated their power, enabling them to immobilize transportation through job actions that paralyzed the Argentine economy.

Workers with different qualifications and skill sets operated, maintained, and cleaned merchant ships—large steamers, sailboats, tugboats, and the many smaller ships that sailed through the Bahía de la Plata or operated in the Buenos Aires interior.

Labor on ships was divided into categories, with functions and titles that differentiated officers from crew. The captain and officers constituted the top of the onboard hierarchy. Job categories also spatially organized steamships into distinct sections: engine room, kitchen, and deck. Firemen, shovelers, oilers, and machinists toiled in the engine room supervised by officers. Cooks and waiters labored in the kitchen, while boatmen and deck hands worked on the upper decks. Despite these job roles, workers routinely performed tasks that required multiple qualifications or skills. When there was work to be done, the crew available completed the tasks. Working conditions and types of labor on board river and coastal steamships did not differ significantly from transoceanic cargo ships and ocean liners, it was more a difference in scale.

Many maritime workers were immigrants, especially onboard workers, and this international dimension added to the mobile character of their workplace. In 1895, 65 percent of workers on vessels in Argentina were foreign-born. In 1905, the Sociedad de Resistencia de Marineros y Foguistas (Resistance Society of Sailors and Firemen, SRMF) reported 144 new members, of whom 47 were Italians, 34 Spanish (mostly Galician), and 26 Argentine. In 1908, the average crew registered by the prefecture reached 45 percent Italians, 15 percent Spanish, and another 15 percent citizens of the Austro-Hungarian Empire.[15] The Coastal Act of 1910 sought to protect the position of Argentinians by reserving coastal and river navigation between inland ports for nationally flagged vessels with an Argentine captain or skipper. For Argentine-flagged vessels it waived certain fees for entry and consular visas at national ports and in some ports in neighboring countries. The act also required a quarter of each crew to be Argentine citizens.[16]

Workers embarked on merchant ships belonging primarily to Argentine-flagged companies, sailing along the Argentine coast and rivers, and the neighboring countries of Brazil,

Paraguay, and Uruguay. These ships came from places as diverse as Mato Grosso, Asunción, the Alto Paraná, towns and cities of Argentina's littoral region, Montevideo and other Uruguayan ports, and Patagonia. Many smaller vessels operated within the port, inter-shipping goods, passengers, and crew.

The travel of workers on board vessels contributed to their international outlook. Sailors transited to and from Uruguay, Paraguay, Brazil, and Argentina, traversing geographical and political borders. Their journeys weakened their perception of these divisions, helping to consolidate a regional space that transcended national borders, and turned the sailors into international workers par excellence. The dual status of migrants and workers on board allowed for a more immediate perception of belonging to a group of people without borders, bound together through their community and shared exploitation. Many workers developed an internationalism, which gave rise to a class identity that could be in tension with professional, ethnic, cultural, or national identities.[17]

Their position at an economic chokepoint, their international composition, and their shared experiences on the job combined to increase the strength of workers. Workers realized the power they possessed through their collective action at such a strategically important location of Argentina's economy. Edgardo Bilsky notes of the Río de la Plata and its main port, Buenos Aires, "To dominate the communication routes, the port for instance, is to dominate the flow of economic life."[18] Workers forged regional, national, and international connections that they drew from intense conflicts with their employers.

Agencia de Colocaciones

de ROSENDO BESADA TORRES - Corrientes, 876

SE OFRECEN BUENOS PEONES, MATRIMONIOS,
DEPENDIENTES DE ALMACEN, MOZOS DE CAFÉ,
CONFITERÍA, HOTEL Y RESTAURANT, COCINE-
ROS PARA CASA PARTICULAR, HOTEL, PARA
CAPITAL Y CAMPAÑA, MUCAMOS, PORTEROS,
CHAUFFEURS, COCHEROS, PANADEROS, MAES-
TROS DE PALA, AYUDANTES, ESTIBADORES,
AMASADORES, MAQUINEROS, APRENDICES, PEO-
NES PARA CASAS DE NEGOCIO, JARDINEROS,
QUINTEROS, DEPENDIENTES DE ESCRITORIO,
TENEDORES DE LIBROS, OFICIALES CARPINTE-
ROS, HERREROS, PELUQUEROS Y TODO SERVI-
CIO PARA LA CAPITAL Y CAMPAÑA, CON BUE-
NAS REFERENCIAS. — — — — — — —

NOTA.—Esta acreditada agencia no cobra remuneración á los
patrones por esta gente que ofrece. Se reciben órdenes por carta ó
Cooperativa Telefónica, 422 (Central). Unión Telefónica, 1107
(Libertad).

Almanaque Gallego, Buenos Aires, 1913

Source: Arquivo da Emigración Galega, Consello da Cultura Galega (Archive of Galician Emigration, Galician Culture Council).

Anarchists and socialists at sea and in the ports

Workers all along the Río de la Plata, particularly in Buenos
Aires and Montevideo, fostered regional, national, and international solidarity networks that supported their struggle
against capitalism and the state. Neighborhoods and community played an essential role in the development of the maritime
labor movement.[19] The residents of La Boca, on the southern
edge of Buenos Aires, turned their community into a center of
intense social and cultural interaction that gave rise to a strong
anarchist movement. Ships carrying people and goods arrived
daily from Argentine provinces and foreign countries before
passengers and cargo transited through the port and riverside

community. The historian Geoffroy de Laforcade characterizes La Boca as a "city apart," by which he means that during the first decade of the twentieth century its geography, surrounded by coasts and dams, with ethnically diverse residents, gave it a distinct character from other neighborhoods. At that time, the port district had transportation connections to other parts of the city, including tram and railway service. It also had its own institutions, including the first firefighting unit in Argentina (fires were frequent in wooden buildings that were home to precarious working-class Argentinians).[20]

The international mobility of this labor force also contributed to the paths of their labor organizing. Most onboard workers were migrants. Maritime laborers had at least a regional experience, but they often crossed national borders in South America. Winston James explores similar connections among Caribbean migrants to the United States and the interactions from their convergence in alternative geographical spaces.[21] Workers on commercial vessels navigating between points in Uruguay, Paraguay, Brazil, and Argentina transited through geographical and political borders. Their crossings weakened the divisive power of distance and states and turned sailors into truly international workers. Neto de Oliveira argues that international mobility supported these workers' development of internationalist positions by illustrating possibilities to them. Working-class internationalism existed in tension with other ways that workers and residents understood their place in the world and in relationship to other people. Trades and professions, ethnicity, culture, and nationality had been constraints on identity, but these factors would prove malleable in the early years of the twentieth century.[22] The fluid status of migrants and workers on ships allowed for a more immediate perception of belonging to a group without borders, sharing a common existence and exploitation.

The many migrants arriving in Argentina from Italy and Spain beginning in the late-nineteenth century traveled through this period's globalizing economic networks and contributed to the internationalism of workers. One of the regional circuits facilitating the dissemination of anarchism consisted of the Río de la Plata port cities, from Buenos Aires to Corumbá, and the Uruguayan, Paraguayan, and Brazilian shores. In this space, organizers such as Constante Carballo accelerated the organization of different anarchist-oriented resistance societies among longshoremen, sailors, and related workers from Argentine ports such as San Nicolás, Ramallo, La Ensenada, and Bahía Blanca, as well as Montevideo, Uruguay, and Asunción, Paraguay. The Argentine groups founded the anarchist Federación Obrera Regional Argentina (FORA) in 1901.

Organized maritime workers demanded salary increases, reduced working hours, and improvements to working conditions. However, their persistent mobilization could only be supported by establishing solidarity networks and the active coordination of resistance societies in different trades and locations. This mobilization became fundamental to the effectiveness of anarchist activities in the region. This is why anarchists established solidarity pacts with other movements in Argentina's interior ports and across the bay in Uruguay to defend union workers and promote union autonomy, union societies (for hiring), workers' education, direct action, ethnic diversity in unions, and antistate revolutionary traditions. Geoffroy de Laforcade argues that these societies exerted a strong influence on the labor movement for several decades, giving rise to the traditions of federalism, solidarity, and autonomy that were passed on to an even more powerful trade union movement—with which they occasionally clashed—after World War I.[23]

Sailors and dockworkers took significant steps forward in their organizing during the period of economic restructuring in the late-nineteenth century. Two periods of direct conflict stand out among decades of tension between workers and capital. Sailors in the Río de la Plata first mobilized in 1888 to demand a wage increase. In 1895, the ever-simmering issue resurfaced, and four thousand workers walked off the job during the first fifteen days of January. The workers had weathered an economic downturn and timed their action during a period of recovery, with the goal of increasing wages and reducing work hours. The Sociedad de Resistencia y Protección Mutua de los Marineros (Society of Resistance and Mutual Protection of Sailors), the first maritime union in Argentina, formed through this agitation.

The two labor conflicts centered on port work and shared many similarities, such as workers drawing strength from their strong community ties in La Boca. Their sense of community helped them organize across distinct crafts and different employers through collective mobilization. Their sense of common work and life experiences in their neighborhood undergirded their solidarity. Although workers lost both confrontations, organizing increased throughout Buenos Aires after 1888, and together these events contributed to worker strength, solidarity, and organizing going forward.

Strong craft societies in the city supported the 1895 strike at the port, fed by a sense of shared working-class experiences by workers and residents. The state directly intervened in the 1895 conflict in ways it did not in 1888. The interior minister, the police chief, and the maritime prefect supported the business owners that associated through the Centro Marítimo (Maritime Center) to break worker resistance in 1895. The leading ship owner, Nicolás Mihanovich, drove the business-political cooperation and collusion, out of which formed the Centro Nacional Costero (National Coastal Center) that aimed to concentrate corporate and political power against workers. Militant socialists, anarchists, and trade unionists continued to organize and form resistance organizations despite not winning the results they desired through job actions in 1895. Organizing can be traced through the lives and organizing of individual workers.

Gabriel Abad worked as a fireman and contributed to the anarchist newspaper *La Unión Obrera*. Originally from Ferrol in Galicia, Spain, he arrived in Buenos Aires in 1885 and immediately connected with anarchists in the city.[24] He belonged to the individualist anarchist group 18 Marzo that formed to commemorate the anniversary of the Paris Commune, and he spoke at a ceremony in February 1893 at the Sociedad San Martin Hall. During his time at the podium, Abad reflected on the revolutionary processes in 1789, 1793, and 1848, when, in his view, bourgeois interests deceived workers, while in the Paris Commune of 1871 he saw a flourishing of workers' interests like never before. Abad was also a correspondent for Barcelona's anarchist newspaper *El Productor* at the time. His agitating attracted the attention of local authorities. Police arrested him in 1899 for distributing a pamphlet titled *Manifiesto de Barracas* during a strike of carpenters and brick layers. Two anarchist groups, Tierra y Libertad and 11 de Noviembre, signed the manifesto. A few days after his arrest Abad, released, went into temporary exile in Montevideo where he connected with another Spanish anarchist, Rafael Roca, and the two edited *La Voz del Trabajador*.

Abad soon returned to Buenos Aires and participated in the May 1890 inauguration of the newspaper *El Perseguido*, through which he engaged in sharp polemics against Argentina's German immigrant socialists over the "social question."[25] However, Abad abandoned his anarchist positions in 1892 and shifted to the socialist outlook that he had criticized in the newspaper. His anarchist peers publicly accused him of being opportunistic or having been a bon vivant during his time in the anarchist movement.[26] It seems that his close relationship with the socialist leader Adrián Patroni influenced his ideological transition. Patroni strongly supported socialist resistance societies against the "intellectualist" theses proposed by Argentine Social Democrats who were largely immigrants from Germany and France.

Abad quickly integrated himself in this political constellation. He participated in the founding of the Sociedad de Herreros,

Gabriel Abad

Source: *La Vanguardia*, Buenos Aires, 1934. Biblioteca CeDInCI (Centro de Documentación e Investigación de la Cultura de Izquierdas, Center of Documentation and Investigation of the Culture of the Left), Buenos Aires, Argentina.

Mecánicos, Fundidores y Anexos (Society of Blacksmiths, Mechanics, Smelters, and Ancillary Workers) in April 1894 along socialist lines. Socialists supplemented on-the-ground organizing with the printed page. They advertized meetings about forming this society in flyers and the socialist newspaper *La Vanguardia*, and even some commercial newspapers supported craft organizing, an important distinction between socialists and anarchists.[27] In June 1894, Abad participated in the meetings at which the new group formulated its constitution. The following year he appeared as a speaker at a May 1 rally and during an event at the socialist Vorwärts Club founded by German immigrants. That same year he cofounded the Barracas Socialist Center.[28]

Abad rose to hold a significant position among socialists in Buenos Aires. The Socialist Party nominated him to stand for parliamentary elections in March 1896, the first time the party nominated candidates. Abad participated in the Argentine Socialist Party Congress in June 1896 as a delegate of the Society of Mechanics that he had helped found.[29] He continued organizing in the years that followed and attended the first and only congress of Socialist Workers' Federation organized by the Socialist Party, as a delegate of the Socialist Center of San Cristóbal (Santa Fe).[30]

Gabriel Abad and Adrián Patroni were well entrenched in the socialist movement during the labor agitation of 1895. Dockworkers agreed to a work stoppage on the first day of the new year. Two days later the sailors joined, which paralyzed the port and the docks. The action coincided with harvest season, the busiest time at the port, when there was an influx of temporary workers.

Socialists played an active role in mobilization. The Socialist Party organ *La Vanguardia* credited socialist militants for the birth of the Sociedad de Herreros, Mecánicos, Fundidores y Anexos. Patroni was the socialist leader most closely identified with the dockworkers and sailors. Although he was a painter, not a maritime worker, the strikers nonetheless elected him as one of their three representatives to negotiate with business owners.[31] There is limited information about Abad's activities during the strike. He was a fireman by trade and probably participated. There are surviving records documenting Abad's participation in a strike in the spring of 1896 when he represented boilermakers integrated into the Sociedad de Herreros, Mecánicos, Fundidores y Anexos.

In balance, socialists were a minority presence on docks, overshadowed by FORA, the anarchist communist organization that the vast majority of dockworkers, longshore workers, and sailors affiliated with.[32] However, ideological differences did not divide the community. Everyday life was far less sectarian than one might expect from staunch political and doctrinal rivals, and community interactions remained functional and even mutually supportive. Anarchists and socialists regularly shared meeting places and overlapped in constituencies, and groups often collaborated to coordinate strikes.

Resistance societies

In the waning years of the First International, luminaries of the anti-authoritarian Left met at the Saint-Imier Congress in Switzerland in 1872 to organize an alternative way forward for international organizing. The delegates in attendance agreed that workers should use strikes as tools to destroy political power and that they should not focus on achieving narrow economic objectives through their struggles. Workers, it was agreed, should rely on direct economic action organized through autonomous federations. Laforcade writes of the congress, "The Bakuninist belief in the spontaneous freedom of individuals living collectively was replaced by the organizational principles of "anarchist communism"—the key influence in Argentine anarchism, one that represented a continuation of Bakunin's social doctrine while modifying its tactical precepts."[33] Mikhail Bakunin and Errico Malatesta both attended the conference, along with members of the Jura Federation and others.

Malatesta personally carried these ideas across the Atlantic and put them forth during his stay in Buenos Aires between 1885 and 1889. He promoted resistance societies and union activity not mired in bureaucracy or narrowly focused on incremental economic gains for workers. Malatesta prioritized general strikes, economic sabotage (direct action), and insurrection as the fundamental mechanisms to advance toward a classless society. He believed in the emancipatory capabilities of all humans, not only of workers, despite identifying workers as the movement's vanguard. He also supported proletarian organizations, provided that certain conditions were met, including the absence of permanent structures of authority; solidarity coordinated through mutual reciprocity; federalism built from the ground up; the community as the only guarantee of true individual freedom; federations of local groups should not be organized through coercion but, rather, open to other forms of association, ideas, and affinities; social order determined by the voluntary aggregation of local and decentralized groups, rather than by formal political structures; and regional and transnational coordination as an instrument to restrict the centralized institutions of oppression and control (that is, the state).[34]

This was the ideological context in which resistance society leaders at Argentine ports creatively adapted European anarchist thought to their local context.[35] The voluntary communal organization of anarchist resistance societies in Argentina, with their dispersed character and small scale, resulted from their efforts. Organizing in Argentina also continued despite discontinuity, drawing strength from their focus on regenerative militant intervention and social change.

Diego Abad de Santillán, whose given name was Sinesio Baudilio García Fernández (1897–1983), was a prominent anarcho-syndicalist militant in Spain and Argentina. He became one of the standard bearers of the Argentine FORA and director of its newspaper, *La Protesta*. Abad de Santillán confirmed the above interpretation of events by lamenting that the regular appearance and disappearance of unions characterized anarchist "gremialismo," a doctrine that advocated for the professional organization of workers in related groups to defend their interests and exercise political influence. Police repression through deportation of prominent militants occurred, but on many occasions this was a product of internal movement dynamics driven by the anarchist movement's anti-authoritarian and decentralizing tendencies. Resistance societies, as defined by the First Congress of Argentine Workers in May 1901, were "workers' collectives organized for the economic struggle of the present" without organic links to the anarchist or socialist movement.[36]

Port workers founded the first anarchist resistance society in 1901 before a major longshore workers' strike. The Catalan immigrant anarchist Francisco Ros had arrived in Buenos Aires in 1897 as a political refugee and was an instigator in the group's formation. La Sociedad de Resistencia de Obreros del Puerto de Capital (Resistance Society of Workers of the Port of the Capital, SROPC) soon became the largest workers' organization in the country. Constante Carballo, "El Galleguito," worked alongside Ros to establish the group. Carballo shared Ros's migrant background. The Galician migrated to Argentina at sixteen and was twenty-six at the time of the group's formation.

The decentralized, federative resistance societies were built on libertarian socialist ideals and conflicted with other ideological currents in the port area of La Boca, such as socialism and Catholicism.[37] The historian Alejandro Belkin argues that trade unionism grew by filling a void with its narrow focus on economic concerns. This resulted in a "division of labor" where each ideological current concentrated on one aspect of worker struggle. Anarchists embodied a maximalist program, socialists directed their energy toward a much less expansive political-electoral program, and trade unions focused on bread-and-butter issues through solidarity and job actions.[38]

On May 25, 1901, around fifty delegates representing thirty-five workers' societies met in Buenos Aires at the founding congress of the Federación Obrera Argentina (Argentine Workers' Federation, FOA). Both socialist and anarchist societies participated in the organization, and it integrated resistance societies of dockworkers, masons, and others. Initially, the Buenos Aires Chamber of Commerce seemed to favor reaching an agreement with workers, but the progressive radicalization of the conflict, the extension of the strike to other sectors, police repression, and pressure from importers from South Africa prevented the final ratification of an agreement, and workers returned to their jobs.[39]

Another strike wave began in early 1902 that paralyzed the Port of Buenos Aires for months and expanded to become a general strike on November 1. Stevedores initiated the strike over the excessive weight of the grain bales they had to carry. It expanded when the FOA joined, followed by warehouse workers in the central market. The job action halted grain exports to Europe and greatly impacted Argentine international trade. The chamber of commerce appointed a commission to negotiate with the strikers, who were represented by Ros and Carballo. The chamber called for an eight-day truce and offered to reduce the size of the grain bales.[40]

In October 1902, Constante Carballo served as treasurer of the Círculo de Enseñanza Libre de la Boca. The group also went by "Amigos de la Enseñanza de la Boca." In August 1902 this organization, which possibly counted a few dozen other Galician immigrants as members, attempted to open two schools. They succeeded in opening one where the principal taught the upper grades, with another teacher in the lower grades. In November they hired an additional teacher, but they closed their doors in late 1902 or early 1903, possibly due to government pressure. Carballo also worked as an agent for the anarchist newspaper

La Protesta Humana, the antecedent of *La Protesta* in his port neighborhood.[41] Community organizing and labor organizing went hand in hand.

The striking workers initially refused the offer from the chamber of commerce, but on November 7 a new assembly of Buenos Aires port workers accepted its terms. The truce lasted only four days.[42] The chamber claimed that accepting the longshoremen's demands would paralyze trade with South Africa. Importers from South Africa demanded ninety-kilogram bags for efficiency (about two hundred pounds) and cared nothing of the human toll it inflicted, given their reliance on Black workers with few labor rights. South Africa was Argentina's seventh-largest trading partner. The annual value of that trade had gone from $8,010 dollars in 1895 to almost $9 million in 1902.[43] This is yet another reminder of the importance of global labor solidarity.

Although the strike was called by dockworkers, other workers linked to the port joined, such as refrigerator workers and fruit workers in the Mercado Central. Representatives from the chamber met with Ros and Carballo to negotiate. The parties reached a principle of agreement that Ros and Carballo planned to present to a general assembly of workers. The agreement envisaged that the heaviest bags, weighing more than seventy kilograms (154 pounds), would be carried by two people and that the bags of wheat would be limited to seventy kilograms.

In the wake of other labor disputes, they canceled the assembly. The refusal of the chamber of commerce to sign the agreement aggravated the situation and helped further radicalize the conflict. The FOA met with police in the port area in a failed attempt to calm the situation. An additional flash point came when the government sent firefighters and sailors to regain control of refrigerated storage from the striking workers. The strike at Campana Refrigerating ended on November 18 with workers returning to their jobs without an agreement.

The strike wave spread to Rosario and Bahía Blanca and to

laborers in Buenos Aires's central fruit market. The mobilization of longshore workers continued, and on November 15 another strike hit the Port of Buenos Aires. The chamber of commerce sought the government's help to end this latest strike by force, demanding shipments of scabs, but too few arrived to replace the striking workers. The chamber also tried to recruit unemployed people in Buenos Aires to scab in the Mercado Central warehouses, but the striking workers convinced them to join their numbers in solidarity. As a stopgap measure, police and firefighters worked in the warehouses but at much slower pace than had been done by the workers out on strike.

Many trade unions supported the strike, including the Federación Nacional de Obreros Constructores de Rodados (National Federation of Road Construction Workers), which signed a solidarity pact with longshoremen. Workers completely stopped port operations with their broad support. They closed the docks, the anchored ships went unattended, and thousands of railcars full of agricultural goods, some perishable, piled up. Stopping trade also hit government coffers by halting customs duties. The broad economic impact of the strike even raised the price of gold.[44]

The strike helped anarchists expand their activity in unions and illustrated the power of the general strike as an instrument for worker struggle.[45] The speed at which the strike spread deeply surprised the anarchists, and the scale of the events went beyond what they envisioned. The historian Yaacov Oved argues that Ros and Carballo's lack of negotiating experience in labor disputes prevented its resolution and increased police and government repression.[46] While the anarchists certainly lacked experience negotiating large labor disputes such as this, the minister of the interior, Joaquín V. González, clearly drove a repressive agenda from the beginning. Strikebreakers carried firearms, and the Argentine government deployed armed forces into Buenos Aires's working-class neighborhoods, marking their first use in a labor conflict in the country. The government declared a state of martial law as troops raided the neighbor-hoods of workers and made mass arrests.

This provided the context for Argentina's Congress to approve the country's first special law to repress the labor move-ment. The Ley de Residencia (Residence Law) authorized the executive branch to deport noncitizens it determined compro-mised national security or acted against public order, without recourse to the judiciary. Over the years the law remained in force, the government applied it primarily to labor organizers and anarchist militants who were immigrants from different parts of the world, although the government occasionally used it to expel immigrant women accused of prostitution.

The government detained Argentinians and deported non-citizens under the Ley de Residencia. Deportations reached five hundred people in the first week. Authorities also intensified the search for anarchists and censored the labor press. The FOA called another strike in response to the deportations. An interlocking cycle of strikes and repression that reached from Buenos Aires to Rosario, La Plata, Campana, and Zárate para-lyzed port activity, workshops, factories, and maritime and rail-way transportation.[47] There was also a bakers' strike that lasted for more than a month, during which authorities raided some bakeries and arrested workers. In a subsequent case, several workers faced prosecution for possessing weapons and bombs. The FOA and a committee representing some fifteen unions drafted a letter to the judge demanding justice and assuring that the defendants did not have weapons. Their actions proved successful, and authorities released the workers.

This cycle gradually declined as the southern summer turned to autumn in 1902, rather than having a clear end point. The most significant legacies of these events resulted from the pas-sage of the Ley de Residencia, which stayed on the books until its repeal in 1958, and the founding of the Sociedad de Resistencia de Marineros y Foguistas in June 1903. This new group unified the societies of sailors, firemen, and other shipboard crew.

On December 16, 1903, Buenos Aires port workers went on strike to demand improvements to working conditions and a reduction in working hours. Sailors and longshoremen protested against loading bales of more than a hundred kilograms. The strike soon radiated to all the activities that made up the heterogeneous port world of the early-twentieth century. Shipyard workers, road workers, and waiters ended up joining a movement that became known as "the big Riachuelo strike" because it lasted two months. The mobilization spread to other cities, almost completely stopping Argentina's port activity again.[48]

During the southern summer of 1903–4, another general strike rocked Argentina. This strike was distinctive due to its dimension and influence both in the communities affected and in the various organizations and spheres of working life.[49] Heavy floods hit and made more visible the poor working-class living conditions on the Riachuelo riverbanks, where the community prepared for Carnival and an election campaign was in full swing. With increasing tensions, the government weighed using the military to preemptively occupy the streets and meeting spaces to prevent a strike.

Port workers, stevedores, drivers, and merchants in Avellaneda to the south of Buenos Aires began the strike, supported by an extensive solidarity network that included the FOA and the Socialist Party.[50] The rolling series of job actions and protests occurred between December 16, 1903, and February 6, 1904. At its peak in January, the strike mobilized more than twelve thousand workers whose families and neighbors supported them. Worker representatives frequently met with government ministers to negotiate a resolution. On January 8, a trade union delegation with broad representation met with Interior Minister Joaquín V. González. González proposed an initiative to draft a labor code.[51]

Strikes reinforced the port community's working-class identity and social ties. The mobilizations also reinforced the solidarity and common action advanced by anticapitalist militants and resistance societies.[52]

Let us now look at the sequence of the conflict, its origins, and the participation of Spanish maritime workers in its configuration.

Constante Carballo, transnational agitator

Police surveillance increased during the strike. In January 1904, Víctor Valle, a former anarchist turned informer known as "el Manchao," wrote a report for the authorities assessing the port area.[53] His nickname translates to "the Spotted," meaning that he probably had a large recognizable birthmark, possibly on his face. In the report, Valle named his contact in the movement as Constante Carballo, the secretary general of the anarchist SROPC, who apparently did not know of Valle's role as a government spy. People had complex identities in the port world and, in any event, informing could be clandestine. Many immigrants and otherwise mobile people also found their home, temporary or not, in the community base that gave the labor and anarchist movement its strength. Trust was essential for movements, but trust could be violated as it was in this case.[54]

Víctor Valle credited the success of the "big strike" to two factors. The first was the geographical scope of the solidarity networks supporting the strike, which included workers from the main Argentine ports and Montevideo. The second was the strong support of the strikers in the port neighborhood. Residents held workers of the SROPC in particularly high esteem, and the group's strength led it to reject police mediation to resolve the conflict.[55] Among the workers who organized and participated in the strike, about five thousand according to estimates at the time, Valle highlighted Carballo, whom he described as an "anarchist and agitator par excellence of the working class, [an] inciter of violence."[56]

42

From the point of view of the authorities, union leaders with anarchist leanings such as Carballo sought to be visible and popular in the proletarian world.[57] The police report highlighted the simplicity of the organization and the security measures around Carballo. The report did not mention internal decision making in the group. Carballo arrived in his role based on neighborhood relations and interpersonal connections formed in the port community, rather than by moving up in hierarchical structures. The police did recognize the collective participation in the protest. Merchants and hoteliers had direct financial reasons to support the workers who were their customer base; the future of their businesses depended on being compensated from the unpaid wages of the striking workers. These local businesses had a stake in the result of this contest between capital and labor, and it became a neighborhood cause. That is why, according to Valle, "almost all strikers based in La Boca enjoy[ed] a certain credit with regard to basic necessities, credit acquired mostly by having fulfilled commitments acquired with previous movements."[58]

Referring to the decision to reject the police arbitration in the port conflict, Valle told Carballo, "[The tone you used] provided a glimpse of your total hatred against any person who represents authority or conflicts in your plans and purposes."[59] Valle saw two factors that could work in tandem to end the conflict at the port in favor of capital and the state. First, the striking workers needed to be exhausted to break their solidarity. Second, the government needed to expel noncitizens under the provisions of the Ley de Residencia. Leaders who made "sensational and violent speeches" that united the working class should be especially targeted for deportation, he believed.[60]

The strike ended in the defeat of the workers. On February 6, 1904, longshore workers voted to return to work. The mass action that brought port operations to a halt, however, left a deep impression on the government and the police. The chief of police told a reporter the "refined tactic employed by a conspiracy of port guilds" was sustained by "a given number of professional agitators," some newly arrived immigrants, although he noted the emergence of a "native element." This led José Gregorio Rossi, Argentina's commissioner of investigations, to submit a list of forty-two trade union leaders to the Ministry of the Interior to target for deportation under the Ley de Residencia.[61]

The landowning and industrial sectors controlling the government promoted the Ley de Residencia and inserted in it a series of repressive measures used by the state against anarchists, socialists, and labor organizers across the board. These measures included declaring a state of martial law, raiding of the premises of the Federación Obrera Regional Argentina and the Socialist Party, seizing newspapers such as *La Vanguardia* and *La Protesta*, and repressing strikes and demonstrations through arrests and deportations.

Commissioner Rossi advocated for deportation orders during the port conflict. These records allow us to understand Constante Carballo in some depth. Evidence of Carballo's organizing skills can be seen in the 1904 application for his expulsion. The interior minister formally applied for Carballo's deportation after the police filed their report. Guided by their informant, police viewed Carballo as "intelligent and astute" and asserted that through his "prestige" he managed the SROPC "at will." Police located the "soul and axis of all subversive movements" in that resistance society and expressed surprise by its capacity to confuse authorities. Rossi wanted to arrest and deport Carballo as soon as possible, but Carballo astutely went to the press, seeking to protect himself by portraying himself as a victim.[62] Rossi viewed Carballo's strong influence as coming from his ability to nurture relationships and foster collaborations.

Authorities also targeted another Spaniard, Andrés Freire, known as "La Coruña," a longshoreman at the Port of Campana, in the deportation application. Police reports referred to him as a "convinced anarchist" in the SROPC. The police chief presented Freire and others in his report as "mere instruments of Carballo," dedicated to denouncing scabs and protecting workers. Despite the insistence of police headquarters, the interior minister rejected deporting Carballo and his comrades, for reasons unclear in the historical record. After the decision, Rossi predicted that anarchists would remain "gravitating about industry and work" ("*gravitando sobre la industria y el trabajo*") with "their usual consequences."[63]

Defeat of the striking port workers in 1904 by government and business failed to slow labor organizing. Rather, this defeat helped propel organizing internationally. Port workers were realizing their true power, as the experience of joint action by workers across the different trades and areas of port operations deeply impacted their sense of solidarity. Looking to move their organizing forward, the anarchist newspaper *La Protesta* announced that the third Congreso Regional de Estibadores (Regional Congress of Stevedores), where port workers from Montevideo would join with their Argentine "compañeros," would be held in Rosario in August 1904.[64]

Despite high expectations and excitement, the congress failed quite dramatically. Several delegates withdrew in the middle of the gathering, including Constante Carballo, who participated in his capacity as representative of the Buenos Aires port workers. Those attending presented conflicting analyses of their defeat that summer. Carballo argued in *La Protesta* after the congress, in September 1904, that the conflict stemmed from the refusal of the dockworkers in Buenos Aires to accept the proposal made by one of the two dockworker organizations in Rosario for an outside person supported by Democracia Cristiana (Christian Democracy) to serve as congress president. Carballo wrote that maritime agents, contractors, and various politicians financed the Christian society. The refusal of the society to withdraw their proposed candidate, rather than the personal threats against Carballo during the dispute, caused most of the groups present, anarchist or not, to abandon the congress. Carballo wrote, "We withdrew when we became convinced that there was nothing possible to do that would benefit the working class."[65] The reality of the situation is that anarchists and trade unionists were deeply divided as to tactics and strategy for working-class organizing and resistance. These differences dogged maritime organizing for decades.

Buenos Aires workers took the initiative after the lack of agreement to promote another meeting, this time in their city. Carballo, Freire, and other dockworkers toured ports in Campana, Zárate, Baradero, San Pedro, San Nicolás, Villa Constitución, and Rosario, speaking to workers. By all accounts it was a successful tour, and port workers looked toward the possibility of a new strike action in November.[66] The libertarian strand of organizing spread during these years. The social conflict percolating in Argentine ports among maritime workers, notably the Spanish immigrant anarchists among them, continued its transnational spread. Porteño workers collaborated with workers in southern Brazil, especially those in Rio de Janeiro.

On October 15 a delegation of maritime workers from Rio, the capital of Brazil at the time, arrived in Buenos Aires. The most prominent worker in the group was the fireman Cândido João dos Santos, whom the Brazilian press considered the "official orator" of the Sociedade Uniao dos Foguistas (Union Society of Firemen). The purpose of the visit was to sign a solidarity pact between the dockworkers of both cities. According to *La Protesta*, the Brazilian delegates visited the newspaper's editorial office and dockworkers' headquarters, in addition to road workers', sailors', and firemen's associations. *La Protesta* expressed enthusiasm: "Relations of solidarity will thus be established between Argentina and Brazil societies, entering an era of cordiality and common struggles very favorable for the international proletarian movement."[67]

A few days later, Constante Carballo and Manuel Vázquez travelled to Rio de Janeiro to participate in a series of activities organized by the Uniao dos Operarios Estivadores (Stevedores Operators Union).[68] The pair participated in their capacities as secretary general of the Sociedad de Resistencia de los Estibadores de Buenos Aires (Resistance Society of Stevedores of Buenos Aires) and secretary of FORA respectively. Rio de Janeiro's *Gazeta de Notícias* covered the meeting in detail, which indicates its importance, as the paper had a conservative republican business perspective. The journalist covering the gathering wrote that Carballo invited dockworkers in Rio de Janeiro with "a firm voice and eloquence" to follow Buenos Aires's example of port organizing and strikes yielding results.[69] Its lack of success notwithstanding, Carballo used the example of Argentina's "big strike" as a paradigm for advancing solidarity among workers in South American Atlantic ports.

Carballo advanced a three-point vision of a workers' pact. First, stevedore unions in Rio de Janeiro and Buenos Aires, he said, should declare themselves "in solidarity in all their conflicts and struggles against capital." The second point called for immediate communication between the unions to facilitate joint strikes or boycotts against steamers, with the idea of extending mobilizations beyond national borders. Finally, the stevedores' union in Rio de Janeiro should attempt "to organize all Brazilian port workers into resistance societies" and seek "their adherence to the present pact." The SROPC worked to bring all stevedores in Argentine and Uruguayan ports into the pact.[70]

In a detailed chronicle of the assembly held on October 22, the *Gazeta de Notícias* noted that the Salón del Casino Comercial (Commercial Casino Hall) was "full of longshoremen and members of various working-class factions." Portraits of the two Argentine leaders illustrated the article. Carballo and Vázquez extended their stay in Rio for another busy day. They toured Guanabara Bay to study its port labor system and talk with coal loaders and other maritime workers. They delivered a lecture at the Casino Español (Spanish Casino), this time with

Vázquez serving as the main speaker. They also continued to talk to the local press.[71]

The Buenos Aires libertarian press praised the level of attention paid to Carballo and Vázquez in Rio de Janeiro. The publishers of *La Protesta* hoped their successful journey anticipated a not-too-distant future that would bring "the victory of labor over exploitative and antihuman capital."[72] Back in Buenos Aires, Carballo continued to organize toward making the pact among South American dockworkers substantial.

In a meeting at La Boca's Teatro Verdi with longshore and other workers, Carballo affirmed his view that workers would carry recent port struggles into the future. "Everything that is to combat the capital that exploits us, everything that tends to improve working conditions," Carballo proclaimed, "will always find the most selfless support in capital's port workers."[73] According to Abad de Santillán, on June 22, 1905, the Comité de Relaciones de la Federación de Estibadores (Committee of Relations of the Stevedores Federation) circulated a document among other societies to form the Federación de Transportes Marítimos y Terrestres (Federation of Maritime and Land Transport) of stevedores and all societies of transportation workers in South America. Organizers planned to inaugurate the federation in a congress to be held in Montevideo in the first half of October of that year, with the participation of the maritime and land transport workers of Argentina, Brazil, Uruguay, Chile, Peru, Paraguay, Ecuador, Venezuela, and Mexico. The congress's goals would be to approve the South American pact, deliberate on the best way to counteract "the advances of absorbing capitalism," and enter a relationship with the International Transport Workers' Federation, a global democratic labor federation founded in London in 1896.[74]

A few days after the Teatro Verdi assembly, police killed three workers in a confrontation with striking longshoremen in Rosario. In response, FORA declared a general strike that would start in the beginning of December, but other job actions kicked off before the general strike began. Longshore workers, refrigerator operators, and machine personnel walked out, demanding the reinstatement of crews in La Boca. Firms temporarily employed these crews to load and unload shipments at the port, depending on the needs of the shipping companies, and apparently dismissed them without cause. Workers also demanded a salary increase.[75] The strike quickly spread to workers at several other companies in the southern Barracas neighborhood.

An article in *La Protesta* with the headline "Triunfo en el Frigorífico La Blanca" ("Triumph at La Blanca Refrigerator") said, "[The strike] has ended today after obstinate resistance on the part of the bosses." The company eventually called a commission to negotiate with the striking workers. The workers appointed Carballo to represent them, and, after two hours of negotiating, the company accepted the conditions stipulated by the workers.[76] The broader strike ended a week later, on November 24, when management agreed to negotiate through another commission representing workers that again included Carballo in his position as secretary of the Sociedad de Resistencia de los Obreros del Puerto.[77] The next day, the two sides came together, and *La Protesta* published the final conditions. Workers won an eight-hour work day, instead of fourteen hours, and a significant wage increase for longshore, warehouse, and the other workers. The agreement guaranteed a half-day wage for those workers who suffered industrial accidents. The agreement also stipulated that a worker who suffered a serious accident was entitled to half salary for three months. They also received assurances that there would be no dismissals of workers for participating in the strike.[78]

This strike wave increased tension in the port, and police continued to focus their attention on workers. The general strike called for December 1–2 to protest the murder of the four workers in Rosario kicked off as scheduled. The same day *Revista de la Policía* (Police Magazine) devoted an article to analysis of the strikes. While the article recognized the need for new legislation to protect workers, the authors stressed that a core group of agitators ultimately lay behind the strength of the unrest.[79] This strike, which had conditional socialist support, hit Buenos Aires and its port the hardest. The government mobilized troops and ordered the Argentine Navy warship *Maipú* to anchor in the port with its guns pointing toward the city. Dockworkers held strong in the face of these threats. According to an article in *La Protesta*, only emptiness, immobility, and "lifeless houses" could be seen, as workers struck and the usually bustling neighborhood ground to a halt.[80]

Popular imagery associated the struggles of 1904 with the presence of the "empresarios de huelgas" (literally "strike entrepreneurs," but its use suggests "strike hustlers"), as union agitators were known in the anti-labor press.[81] Predictably, the declaration of the general strike triggered a barrage of critical comments. At first, attention focused on alleged intimidation by strikers of workers still on the job, "trying by all possible means to convince those who were continuing to work." As the conflict deepened, the remarks soon turned more hostile, directed against the "disturbing elements" and the "strike bosses," accusing organizers of not having jobs themselves.[82] Responding to a complaint in the evening newspaper *El Diario* alleging the absence of genuine workers on the FORA Federal Council, all its members published a reply in January 1905 indicating their workplaces.[83] This public transparency soon facilitated police repression.

On February 4, 1905, a group of civilians and soldiers commanded by the Unión Cívica Radical (Radical Civic Union, UCR) revolted against the government of President Manuel Quintana. Although anarchists were not involved in the uprising, the government declared martial law for a month and seized the opportunity to arrest a large group of labor organizers. The government held forty-eight people, including Carballo, for almost two weeks on the *Maipú* before deporting them to Montevideo. The government silenced *La Protesta*, but the anarchist newspaper

El Obrero in Montevideo continued and published an article detailing Carballo's arrest while he was alone in the port area.[84]

Few sources survive documenting Carballo's experiences during detention and deportation. Authorities also deported his comrade Francisco Corney, a machinist and union leader on the *Maipú*. Corney kept a notebook later preserved by his family that lets us see into these events from his perspective. He wrote that police arrested him on Tuesday, February 7, at nine in the morning at his home in La Boca, deprived him of his belongings, and imprisoned him on the *Maipú* along with the other deportees. The next day authorities transferred him and the other prisoners to the commercial steamer *Helios* to cross the Río de la Plata to Montevideo.[85]

Another deportee, the anarchist Alberto Ghiraldo, wrote about these deportations in his book *La Tiranía del Frac*, in which he recorded profiles of deportees, including some of those on the *Maipú*. Ghiraldo described Carballo as an "enthusiastic unionist, whose effective action [was] felt, mainly, within the dockworkers" and as "the black beast of the La Boca police, maritime agents, and fruit exporters."[86] Ghiraldo also wrote a short biography of Francisco Corney.

Corney was born in Barcelona in 1874 and arrived in Buenos Aires in 1900. A FORA affiliate, he became a member of its Federal Council in 1904. Corney contributed to the labor press in Buenos Aires, frequently using the pseudonym "Germinal," a common reference in radical circles to Émile Zola's novel with that title. Authorities arrested him and deported him to Montevideo in February 1905. He quickly returned to Buenos Aires at the request of the FORA, but a subsequent arrest and deportation led him to settle in Uruguay in June 1905.

The writings of Alberto Ghiraldo and Francisco Corney allow us to understand the deportation process and the place that Montevideo and other locations in this radical geography occupied in the broader space of Atlantic anarchist connections. Since the adoption of the Ley de Residencia at the end of 1902,

Constante Carballo

Source: "Os estivadores," *Gazeta de Notícias*, Rio de Janeiro, October 23, 1904, Collection of the National Library Foundation, Brazil.

police in Buenos Aires observed with concern that anarchists who had been expelled from Buenos Aires took advantage of their ship's port call in Montevideo to disembark and enter Uruguay rather than continuing to their supposed final destination. This led José Gregorio Rossi, Argentina's commissioner of investigations, to consider the capital of Uruguay the "most dangerous headquarters for anarchism."[87]

Anarchists transformed the proximity of the two cities into a circuit of exchange in their attempts to circumvent government expulsion. From the police perspective, "the immensity of [the] coasts" made "the surveillance of clandestine re-entry impossible," facilitating the permanent flow of anarchists.[88] The enforcement of the Ley de Residencia through deportations contributed to the territorial expansion of anarchism, rather than its intended effect of eradicating it, by expanding networks of solidarity and liberatory actions across state borders. The state-level actions combined with grassroots interpersonal connections, such as those created by Carballo's propaganda tour through the ports of Buenos Aires, Rosario, and Rio de Janeiro in February 1905, to create a strong solidarity network. The repressive approach of Argentina's government turned it into a kind of "Río de la Platist" version of Russian tsarism, while Montevideo remained a beacon of freedom to anarchists, though this was certainly not absolute.

Authorities initially expelled Carballo from Argentina in February 1905. Police arrested him again in July, five months later. The Rio de Janeiro periodical *O Século* included a telegraph from Argentina warning that police had just arrested the "dangerous anarchist" Constante Carballo for violating the banishment to which he had been sentenced.[89] He emerged months later in Montevideo, which suggests that he had been deported once again. After his first deportation, Carballo entered Argentina five more times clandestinely, and as many times authorities deported him.[90] A letter from the Argentine diplomatic consul in Montevideo noted that Carballo lived in the port area of Montevideo in early 1906.[91] Through his repeated deportations and stays in Montevideo, Carballo again reemerged in Buenos Aires in September 1906.

An article in *La Protesta* announced that a group of deportees had returned to Buenos Aires as delegates to the Congreso de Librepensamiento (Freethought Congress). The Montevideo anarchist newspaper *La Giustizia* reported immediately after the congress's inauguration that police had arrested and deported Carballo.[92] *La Protesta* reported in 1907, without apparent surprise, that Carballo had been arrested yet again, while strolling through the Buenos Aires port area, and deported.[93] The anarchist newspaper expressed, with irony, its conviction that the Argentine government was doing Carballo a favor. By this time, Carballo had settled in the Uruguayan capital and, according to the publishers, he had to thank the Argentine government for this "official attention, worthy of gratitude, for paying for the comrade's return trip."[94]

A few days later, the Montevideo press announced that Carballo, "famous libertarian propagandist," had arrived back in the city aboard the steamer *Colombia* and that, because of communication between the police of both countries, he was going to be arrested by the Uruguayan police and sent back to Buenos Aires. The next day he was back in Buenos Aires, and, from that point on, Carballo's personal struggle against the state transformed into "the Carballo case," a focal point of anarchist struggle against the state. Montevideo, a port city that had been a place of refuge in the past, became part of the geography hostile to anarchism, along with Buenos Aires, Sao Paulo, and Rio de Janeiro.[95] This turn of events provoked a strong reaction from the anarchist press in Montevideo and Buenos Aires, which chronicled protests, solidarity campaigns, and subscription lists to support their comrade, a victim of state repression.[96]

Meanwhile, Carballo seemed to attempt to keep a low profile and avoided direct confrontation with Argentine authorities. The Galician anarchist posted a letter to the minister of the interior,

Manuel Montes de Oca, on July 29, 1907, almost two weeks after his return to Buenos Aires. In the letter, Carballo requested his freedom and promised not to participate "in any kind of propaganda, either of advanced ideas, or in favor of strikes." He also wrote that he would only work to "honestly" meet the needs of his family, especially his mother, who was very sick. He promised to withdraw from organizing and accept his future deportation if he took it up again.[97]

We do not know if Carballo intended to follow through with this course of action because authorities rejected his offer. The government deported him in February 1905 for "being one of the most effective and recalcitrant agitators of port crafts" and for his numerous returns after previous deportations. This measure was taken despite the fact that, as the interior minister's report recognized, every time Carballo returned clandestinely to Buenos Aires, he stayed in the La Boca or Barracas neighborhood with a low profile, without engaging in "agitator activities," attempting to avoid arrest.[98]

There is one final twist to this story. On August 7, 1907, the day of Carballo's scheduled deportation to A Coruña, Spain, via England, authorities released him. The anarchist press noted that this came after the death of his companion that day. There are no remaining records of his life in the radical press or in police and diplomatic archives for the next decade. An article in an anarchist newspaper ten years later reproached him for taking a "bourgeois" job as an "armament captain" in a "shipowner's house," though the article recognized that he had been "tenaciously" persecuted by the police in the past. The article also criticized Carballo for receiving what they claimed was high pay during his two years as secretary of the Sociedad de Estibadores (Stevedores' Society). Despite everything, and even with this concession, the editor harshly criticized Carballo's definitive departure from anarchist militancy.[99]

Similar to many anarchist agitators in other places around the world, Carballo knit together solidarity networks throughout

South America through his travels and organizing. The historian José Aricó writes that much of the success of anarchism in the region was due to the appearance of the "mobile agitator" figure able to join proletarian struggles: "a figure who did not recognize national borders and who moved following a sharp intuition to perceive the signs of conflict."[100] In the world of dockworkers, these mobile agitators were especially dynamic and influential. The solidarity they wove between longshoremen, other port workers, and firemen was strategic, often coming through deportations and artful returns to the places from which authorities removed them by force.

Organizing at Atlantic ports took reticular form similar to the meshed structure of nuclei and neurons in the brain. Carballo's decisions came at great risk to himself and family, limited by laws and the enforcement power of states through the transatlantic geography he and others moved. Sailors and dockworkers enacted the solidarity and information networks, embodying the connections between unions and anarchist militants that struggled against the repression of governments and businesses. In the end, as the contemporary historians Albornoz and Galeano concluded, the militant period of Carballo's life between the mid-1890s and 1907 was but one strand of the network of contacts between the ports of the Rio de la Plata and the Brazilian coast. The untiring organizer was "a piece of the same space and circulation of the Atlantic world of mobile agitators."[101] The strength of this network can be seen through continued organizing after Carballo removed himself from the front lines of radical organizing.

FORA held its sixth congress in Rosario in September 1906. Enrique Taboada (who went by the alias Roque Aída Bonet) and Carlos Fornos, both well-known militant Spanish immigrant trade unionists, presided as representatives of Buenos Aires sailors and firemen. Delegates elected Fornos to FORA's Federal Council as a maritime sector representative. A few months later he served as a delegate to the Liga Obrera Naval Argentina

(Argentine Naval Workers League, LONA) at the first Congreso de Unidad Sindical (Congress of Union Unity), together with Juan Colmeyro, who had been born in Argentina to Galician parents.

Enrique Taboada's travels to and from Argentina marked him personally and connected him to maritime organizing across the continent.[102] Born in the Galician town of A Coruña in 1870, Taboada was a leader in La Cosmopolita, a union of waiters, cooks, and maritime nurses established in 1905. He also a directed the libertarian Germinal group.[103] Taboada probably arrived in Buenos Aires as a maritime waiter on a Mala Real Inglesa ship in late 1905 or early 1906. After crossing the Atlantic he went by the name Roque Aída Banet to obscure his identity from authorities.

He joined FORA soon after his arrival and participated in its sixth congress as a representative of Buenos Aires maritime workers. Taboada travelled to Rosario to agitate among dockworkers in October 1906. Police arrested him on October 11, accusing him of having killed two scabs and for possessing an incendiary device. Authorities released him less than two weeks later, after Rosario police requested telegraphic reports from police in Spain and verified that he did not work as a longshoreman.[104] It appears that sometime in 1907 Taboada returned to Galicia, where he remained linked to maritime unionism. In 1914, he helped found El Despertar Marítimo, an association of sailors, firemen, and skippers from the merchant marine that also attracted merchant navy crew, port workers, and sailors on fishing vessels.[105]

Uruguay: the other shore in the mirror

Uruguay's capital city Montevideo is 130 miles from Buenos Aires and located on the northwest bank of the Río de la Plata. Often overshadowed by its larger neighbor, Montevideo had an advantage that Buenos Aires did not in the form of a natural harbor that allowed deep-draft vessels to dock. Construction to expand and update the shoreside facilities of the port to increase its capacity began in 1901. In addition to new docks and other infrastructure, workers built the 950-meter-long Sarandí breakwater, the new eastern breakwater and city landmark, that extends from a pedestrian street in the city of the same name. The Sarandí breakwater and its western twin formed the sides of a 400-meter-wide access channel to the port of Montevideo, with a depth greater than ten meters for large vessels to access the metropolitan port. Construction crews completed the project in 1909.[106]

Uruguay shared the export-led economic structure of most other Latin American countries at the turn of the century. Its two primary exports were wool and frozen meat destined for Belgium, France, and Argentina. Montevideo's port also served as a cargo redistribution hub. Infrastructure improvements facilitated strong economic growth through grain and livestock exports. In turn, the arrival of immigrants—notably from Italy and Spain—greatly expanded Montevideo's and Uruguay's population. Authorities did not keep accurate statistical data accounting for new arrivals. The vast majority of those arriving from Spain came from Galicia, and this group disproportionately contributed to maritime and port activities.[107] In 1889, Montevideo had a population of 215,061 inhabitants. Approximately 47 percent of the population were foreign nationals. In 1908, the population of the city was 309,231, with 30 percent foreigners. In 1939, the population had grown to 655,389 inhabitants, but we do not know the percentage of foreign-born residents at that time.[108]

Compared to Buenos Aires, Montevideo's port had a similarly long history of labor conflict. In 1896, maritime, river, and port workers walked off the job. The government met the workers with swift and severe repression that included the prohibition of their meetings and the arrest of their leaders, which even brought sympathetic coverage in newspapers not known to be friendly to the cause of labor. The export crisis and the influence of the "porteño" labor movement in Buenos Aires drove a wave of new strikes in 1900 and 1901.[109] It started with a violent work stoppage at the port that expanded to the mobilization of La Teja quarry workers that provided materials for port construction. On August 9, 1901, workers organized in the Sociedad de Resistencia de los Trabajadores de la Construcción del Puerto de Montevideo (Resistance Society of the Workers of the Construction of the Port of Montevideo) sabotaged construction machinery at the port. Police arrested the Galician migrant Ernesto Vila a few days later for his alleged role as a leader of the revolt, along with Iberian immigrants such as José Bares from Pontevedra and José Roura from Mallorca.

While Montevideo and Buenos Aires competed for commercial hegemony in the Bahía de la Plata, solidarity marked maritime and port labor organizing in both cities. The socialists and anarchists organizing the first resistance societies at the Port of Buenos Aires understood that the Río de la Plata was a common area of resistance. Buenos Aires seemed to occupy the leading role. Anarchists from the other shore, whether they arrived through deportation or voluntarily, shaped the struggle in Montevideo. The influence of Buenos Aires–based organizers continued until the 1920s, at which point Uruguay's labor movement took a more autonomous direction.

Dockworkers formed strong relationships that spanned the two ports. For example, the stevedores' congress in Buenos Aires in April 1903 brought together thirty-two delegates representing workers at the Port of Buenos Aires and the other Argentine ports alongside representatives from the Estibadores del Puerto de Montevideo (Stevedores from the Port of Montevideo). Representatives from the Cargadores y Descargadores de Carbón (Coal Loaders and Unloaders) and Estibadores y Trabajadores de Salto Oriental (Stevedores and Workers of Salto Oriental) societies also attended.[110] This relationship remained stable and strong for the next decade.

In May 1905, eleven thousand maritime workers walked out in Montevideo, including longshoremen, firemen, sailors, coopers, machinists, and fishermen, demanding a wage increase and improvements to their working conditions. Two Galician anarchists, Adrián Troitiño and Joaquín Ucha, deported from Argentina through the Ley de Residencia the year prior, represented the workers. The strike faced strong opposition, lasted a month and a half, and benefited from the active solidarity of Buenos Aires dockworkers, who refused to unload the boats coming from Montevideo. It also led to violent clashes in Montevideo's El Cerro neighborhood, with guns fired by strikers, scabs, and police. Constante Carballo also joined the strike effort, representing Buenos Aires stevedores in Montevideo after one of his deportations from Buenos Aires. He shared messages of solidarity from across the river with worker assemblies in Montevideo.[111]

Transition in Buenos Aires

In 1910, the Argentine labor movement in general, but particularly in Buenos Aires, suffered intense state repression through deportations, the use of the police against strikers and protesters, and the adoption of new laws against workers' organization. In this context, between the months of January and March 1910, two key strikes at the port preceded the formation of the Federación Obrera Marítima (Federation of Maritime Workers, FOM). One strike was called by the syndicalist Sociedad de Marineros (Mariners' Society), and the other was convened by the anarchist Sociedad de Foguistas (Firemen's Society).

The mariners' strike ended a few days later through the mediation of the police chief and the signing of a new agreement. However, the firemen rejected the mediation offered by the police chief, and the conflict lasted for two months, culminating in a salary agreement but without improvements in working conditions. According to Laura Caruso, the intransigence weakened the firemen. Already a minority union, the Sociedad de Foguistas soon lost members, a situation aggravated by increasing government repression. The strike victory strengthened the position of the revolutionary syndicalists, which helped consolidate this ideological current among union leaders in the sector. A few days after the firemen's strike ended, workers formed the FOM, a new federated syndicalist organization. Learning the lessons from the strikes led by the Sociedad de Marineros and the Sociedad de Foguistas, maritime leaders increasingly dialogued with government and state institutions to advance worker interests. The FOM continued this practice throughout the 1910s.[112]

The FOM won labor control during strikes between 1916 and 1917, which allowed the FOM to impose a closed shop in the maritime sector. On December 1, 1916, the maritime workers declared a general strike at the Port of Buenos Aires, the first labor action that occurred during the Argentine economic recession caused by the First World War. In the face of falling real and nominal wages, the deterioration of the standard of living, and the terrible working conditions, the assemblies of firemen and sailors from the Port of Buenos Aires drew up a list of demands that appealed to a broad cross section of workers. The shipping companies refused to negotiate, and the workers walked off the job. The conflict came to an end with mediation by the new police chief. The workers agreed to return to their jobs, and the companies agreed to share control of hiring deck crew and machinists with the FOM.[113]

It is likely that many officers and captains joined the FOM in 1910. During the maritime strikes of 1916 and 1917, officers and captains created their own professional organization. In September 1918, the Centro de Capitanes de Ultramar y Oficiales de la Marina Mercante (Center of Overseas Captains and Officers of the Merchant Marine) formed and established a solidarity pact with the FOM. Officers and workers viewed solidarity to be in their mutual interest, to defend union representation of everyone on board. In January 1919, both organizations declared a general strike in the maritime sector, seeking legal recognition and the institutionalization of union control on board ships.[114]

Leading organizers apparently accepted the presence of shipboard hierarchies in the union and later solidarity with the independent Centro de Capitanes. The FOM held significant power in this economic sector, in relation to the state and in the labor movement. The FOM sought to unify the entire maritime sector in the union struggle, regardless of the position or qualification of workers. Revolutionary syndicalists sought to build a single industrial union, with a federated structure that consolidated labor power against the state. This organizational structure increased its ability to support and represent workers when negotiating.[115] This cross-hierarchy solidarity overcame the fragmentation of maritime labor. The FOM brought sailors, firemen, and other shipboard workers together with captains and officers for joint action, dissolving the division of labor on ships in their organizing.

The solidarity pact between the two organizations ruptured in 1924 because of conflicting positions on a retirement law proposed by the government. While the officers, captains, and pilots supported the law along with the shipping company owners, the FOM flatly opposed it and called a general strike against it. Laura Caruso and Gustavo Contreras argue that the law completely ignored the reality of maritime labor. The law required thirty years of work to gain retirement benefits, a level of seniority almost impossible to achieve for workers in the sector, and it required continuous, non-interrupted work. Shipboard work broke down bodies and left "useless men," a "waste," in far less time than the thirty years required for retirement, which was twice the length of time required for officers by the law.[116]

The FOM largely controlled the coordination and organization of workers in the sector, which allowed it to dominate Argentine ports and ships between 1916 and 1921. It monopolized labor supply, mediating the crew supply for vessels, and it controlled the registration of workers able to embark. A general strike in February 1920 in solidarity with other port struggles and against a lockout by the Mihanovich Shipping Company ended with the union victory in March 1921. However, two months later, a new employer and government offensive militarized the Port of Buenos Aires, expelled the FOM workers, and forcibly imposed an open shop.[117]

The growth of the FOM among maritime workers positioned the Consejo Federal (Federal Council) as the leading representative of labor before capital in moments of conflict such as strikes and boycotts. Its strength forced shipping companies to recognize FOM representation even through their frequent challenges to its authority. The FOM created an organizational model that stitched together the fragmented world of maritime work. Sailors, firemen, and other shipboard workers joined, grouped within sections for their various trades and categories (federations) within an industrial union.

The FOM aligned under the political-labor strategy of revolutionary syndicalism.[118] Trade unionists promoted federations as a coherent way to extend union organization quickly and effectively. The federated structure differed greatly from the federations of resistance societies promoted by anarchists in the early years of the twentieth century, including the FORA. The focus of anarchist resistance societies lay outside of direct labor organizing, without the level of pragmatism of this period of syndicalism. The federal structure of revolutionary unions facilitated the rapid organization of sections to overcome the perils of craft organization by trade.

The federation of the different anarchist resistance societies was the form chosen for workers' organization by anarchists at the beginning of the twentieth century. The resistance societies preserved the maximum degree of autonomy for associations

of workers and artisans that sought to be independent from—
and to abolish—the state and capitalism. For its part, the FOM
sought to overcome the divide between professional groups to
grow a union based exclusively on industry. This federal structure grouped trades and categories in the same geographical
region around a branch or sector of activity. This structure concentrated power to a degree, which was difficult for some anarchists but resulted in a strong industrial union until its demise.

Conclusion

During the last decade of the nineteenth century, a succession of
terrorist attacks by anarchists led European states to gather at
the International Anti-Anarchist Conference in Rome in 1898.
Increased international police cooperation was one result. The
prospect of increased repression in Europe provoked alarm
in South America. Governments feared that anarchists persecuted in Europe would move to countries like Brazil, Argentina,
and Uruguay, which had relatively open immigration laws.
Argentina's Ley de Residencia can be interpreted as a response
to that concern.[119] The approaches of South American states to
control or repress anarchists also contributed to the spread of
this ideal and worker internationalism. After Argentina passed
the Ley de Residencia in 1902, Brazil passed a similar law in
1907. The two governments frequently collaborated.

Expulsion laws advanced the internationalization of polic-
ing that came out of the preceding decade of rapprochement
between the police of South America, especially those of Brazil
and Argentina. It resulted in information exchange agreements by post and by telegraph. However, when authorities
used the laws to target anarchists, the police officers monitoring the South American Atlantic had to maneuver within the
sovereign decisions of their own governments, the gaze of the
press, and the impact that each expulsion had in neighboring

countries.[120] In Uruguay, during the first two decades of the twentieth century, legislation prevented people that had not been formally convicted by courts from being required to register. As a result, the government deported fewer people than Argentina. Uruguay's Law 8,868 in 1932 closed the country's long-open doors.

In the next chapter we will see that the process and form of maritime organizing in Argentina did not extend beyond the Southern Cone. In areas to the north such as Cuba, maritime unionism took a distinct ideological and the organizational course. On the island, under the leadership of the Spanish migrant Juan Arévalo, among others, a reformist and "socialist" current developed that combated the influence of anarcho-syndicalism among maritime workers' societies and promoted a Pan-American model, sponsored by the conservative American Federation of Labor (AFL), that moved away from anarchist and syndicalist internationalism.

CHAPTER TWO

The Caribbean Atlantic

Anarchism and Reformist Unionism

Spanish immigrant maritime workers in the Americas tended to organize along anarchist and syndicalist lines. However, in Cuba they worked within reformist union structures that justified tactical collaborations with capital and participated in party politics. This direction of working-class struggle took form through the influence of a Galician emigrant to Puerto Rico, Santiago Iglesias Pantín. He aligned with AFL president Samuel Gompers and helped found the Federación Libre de Trabajadores (Free Federation of Workers, FLT) in 1899. While Pantín was not a maritime worker, his influence is evident in the union model of maritime workers at the Port of Havana during the second decade of the nineteenth century. Another Galician migrant, Juan Arévalo Vieites, even more directly advanced reformist unionism at the Port of Havana and elsewhere in Cuba. This chapter documents maritime organizing in Cuba and its connections throughout the Caribbean and North America.

Economic development and social conflict

The Cuban economy rapidly expanded in the years immediately following its independence from Spain in 1898 until the second US occupation following collapse of Tomás Estrada Palma's government in 1906. Economic growth continued but at a moderate pace influenced by demographic expansion from immigration, political developments inside the country, and international trade. Cuba reached high levels of per capita income compared to other Latin American countries by the beginning of the First World War.[1]

This war, however, was not the health of the Cuban state. The negative impact of the war continued to hurt the island's economy until the global economic crisis in the 1930s. The conflict in Europe increased Cuba's dependence on North American markets and sugar production to the detriment of economic diversification. Increased trade restrictions followed US entry to the war in 1917, and protectionist measures in the United States and Europe after the war's end that lasted into the 1920s increased the impact of market contractions and lessened the benefits of market expansion for sugar. Foreign credit helped balance fluctuations in international trade, while the domestic economy expanded through immigration.[2]

The city of Havana grew through these economic fluctuations, and public works projects reshaped the city and the port. A visible example of these urban changes came in the early-twentieth century as the sugar beet industry in the United States and Europe expanded and put downward pressure on the price of cane sugar, the island's primary export. Cuban producers invested in updating export infrastructure to create new efficiencies at the warehouses and docks to reduce the time and labor it took to bring their product to market. Havana's urban development followed that of English ports such as Blackpool and Brighton. Domestic merchants and landowners as well as US corporations invested in commercial warehouses that eventually expanded beyond the confines of the old port, reshaping the harbor front.

In 1912, Havana's new central train station, La Habana Central, opened on the grounds of the old arsenal near the port. It served as a hub for passenger and freight transport.[3] By then, two thousand ships called at Havana's port annually, which led to port expansion projects. These modernization projects and improvements to coastal navigation combined to reduce transportation costs and integrate the Port of Havana with newly constructed ports in Camagüey and Cienfuegos to the west. Havana's urban growth soon pushed against the expansion of transportation, warehousing, and other infrastructure near the port. Despite improvements, the Port of Havana could not compete with the efficiency of ports in New York and New Orleans. US firms constructed sugar refining factories near these US ports to control this stage of production, preferring to import raw sugar directly to these ports without going through Havana.

Havana and the other Cuban ports processed direct imports and exports, while Cuban shipping companies carried cargo between domestic ports and through the Antilles to Mexico, Panama, and Venezuela. The company Sobrinos de Herrera carried goods and passengers from Havana across the island's north coast and around to Santiago de Cuba. It also had two ships that made regular trips to Santo Domingo, Jamaica, and Puerto Rico.[4] Another company, Empresa de Vuelta Abajo de Antolín y Collado, later Empresa Julián Alonso, operated along the northern coast of the Pinar del Río district and made stopovers in Bahía Honda, Río Blanco, La Esperanza, Dimas, Arroyo de Mantua, and La Fe. These coastal lines (*cayeras*) expanded to meet the needs of merchants with powerful economic and political roles in Cuba. The harvest cycle of export crops (sugar) and imports of European luxury goods for the wealthy, as well as demand for passenger service, drove the expansion of maritime transport.[5]

A number of small companies focused on specific areas. Compañía de Antinogenes Menéndez, later known as Odriozola y Cía, based in Cienfuegos, made crossings along the south coast from Batabanó, with stops in Cienfuegos, Casilda, Tunas de Zaza, Júcaro, Santa Cruz del Sur, Manzanillo, Ensenada de la Mora, and Santiago de Cuba. Other important shipping companies were the Empresa del Ferrocarril de La Habana, which operated along the southern coast of Pinar del Río. Empresa de Vapores Zulueta's steamer, the *Otegüí*, made crossings to Sagua la Grande and Santiago de Cuba, and it sometimes called at ports in Jamaica, Puerto Rico, and Venezuela. Compañía de Vuelta Abajo Steam Ship Company regularly covered the south coast from Pinar del Río to Surgidero de Batabanó.[6]

The new Cuban Republic, established in 1902, approved a series of protectionist measures for the domestic shipping companies to guard against the encroachment of US firms, which included laws restricting coastal trade to ships operated exclusively by Cuban companies. The foreign companies, mostly owned by Spanish citizens, changed the flags of their vessels and the registration of their firms to Cuba. A few US companies, such as the Ward Line and the Munson Steamship Line took advantage of legal gaps and did this with some of their vessels in Cuba to expand into Cuban commercial maritime traffic. Only three Cuban shipping companies remained by 1916, despite this favorable legal framework: Sobrinos de Herrera, Antinógenes Menéndez, and Julián Alonso. The three companies merged that year into the Empresa Naviera de Cuba, with a combined fleet of twenty-seven vessels.[7]

Cuba entered the First World War in April 1917, one day after the United States, when its Senate voted in favor of a declaration of war against Germany in response to continued German U-boat attacks. Most Latin American countries remained neutral in the conflict, but Cuba, Panama, Bolivia, and Uruguay joined the Allies. In June, Cuba nationalized all privately owned Cuban-flagged ships into auxiliary vessels of the navy and prohibited ship owners from changing the national registration of their ships. The government also seized the German ships moored in Cuban ports in August and leased the vessels to Empresa Naviera de Cuba. The government later took command of these vessels after the leasing firm failed to meet its debt obligations. Competition from foreign shipping companies increased in the interwar years.[8]

Migration and community formation

The historian José Antonio Vidal has studied Spanish migrants living in Casablanca, a neighborhood of Havana. This community had roots reaching back to the late-eighteenth century when Galicians from Rías Altas began migrating to the island. José Rivas, a native of Ferrol, opened the first wine bar and restaurant in the neighborhood. By the mid-nineteenth century, several Galician shipowners had settled in Havana. Manuel Suárez and his nephew Francisco Vilar Casteleiro owned an important fishing fleet, shipyards, and one of the largest naval businesses in Cuba in the 1870s. At the end of the nineteenth century, a group of small factories and artisan workshops remained, located in the Casablanca neighborhood, where workers manufactured sails for the sloops and ships that traveled the bay and for the sailboats that still carried out maritime trade. This group of Galician immigrants mostly arrived on the island from the fishing villages of Ares and estuaries of Ferrol, supported through migratory chains of family and friends. Once in Cuba, they formed an ethnic enclave with regional roots in their neighborhood.[9]

Predominantly young, single men migrated, and they later formed families in Cuba through the subsequent migration of Iberian women and also with Cuban women. The Galician community continued to grow and, by the mid-nineteenth century, was one of the most important Spanish-Galician colonies on the island. The men worked on merchant ships, fished, and may have smuggled goods between the United States, Mexico, and Cuba as customs controls were weaker on Cuba's northern coast.

During the US occupation of Cuba between 1898 and 1902, most of these migrants put themselves at the service of the new administration, with the goal of economic reconstruction. Galician ship and shipyard owners, captains, and sailors in the main port towns all contributed to this task. Galicians also formed an enclave in Isabela de Sagua in the years following Cuba's independence in 1903. Sailors and fishermen worked at the port as their neighborhood took form.[10]

In almost all Cuban ports, fishermen, merchant sailors, and even the simple boatmen who transported people or goods across Havana Bay were Galician migrants who formed small enclaves in the sugar ports of Manzanillo, Nuevitas, and Caibarién as well as the fishing towns of Batabanó, La Fe, and Arroyos de Mantua.[11] The massive presence of Spaniards in Cuba is reflected in census data. In 1899, 50.5 percent of Cuban sailors were born in Spain. In Havana, Spaniards accounted for just over 80 percent of all sailors and boatmen, and they comprised 62 percent of fishermen in 1907.[12] Between 1899 and 1919, migrants from Spain never surpassed 9 percent of the total population of Cuba, but they comprised 22 percent of Havana's population. Demographic and migration changes reduced the prominence of Spanish sailors and fishermen toward mid-century, but they remained significantly overrepresented in the industry in relation to population statistics.[13]

Labor organizing

Labor struggles in Cuba in the late 1880s and early 1890s made visible the limits of Spanish colonial reformism. According to Joan Casanovas, the reforms that followed the abolition of slavery in 1886 facilitated the development of the labor movement, but the administration increasingly restricted union activity after 1889. Despite increased repression, the anarchist workers' movement continued to show great capacity for mobilization for a time. Radical unionism continued to grow among workers beyond its base in the tobacco industry and in populations outside Havana. Under these circumstances, anticolonial feelings intensified among the workers, which led to the opening of the labor movement to the left wing of the independence movement.

Anarchists participated in labor struggles in the 1880s to the early 1890s and in the independence movement. The relative freedom of the press in Cuba between 1887 and 1892 allowed the labor and non-separatist republican press to report on the intense labor organizing during these years when anarchists played a key role. Anarchist propaganda in favor of class solidarity and against nationalism lowered support among working-class Spaniards for the island's colonial status. Although most Iberians continued to oppose independence, in the 1890s the anti-independence virulence common in the Spanish-led labor movement decreased, and a large number of Spaniards became separatists, supporting independence.[14]

The organizational proposals, the tactics of workers' struggle, and the political strategy of the first Cuban anarchists were received positively among a wide swath of urban workers on the island. The island's radical print culture became the primary vehicle for a particular form of collectivist anarchism to take root in Cuba. Later, this anarchist current reached migrant worker communities. The uptick of government repression after the mid-1890s, economic and political crisis, and finally the War of Independence (1895–98) all constrained the spread of radicalism in cities and even more so in rural areas. After independence, radical workerist ideals triumphed in the urban sphere and began to spread in rural areas.[15]

During the first two republican decades, dockworkers promoted a series of strikes demanding the restoration of the rates that governed the transportation of goods in Havana (1901) and Cienfuegos (1902). These unions framed their demands as restoring the rights of labor that had been "usurped" by shipping companies and trading houses, mostly with foreign capital. Anarcho-syndicalist groups in Cuba and on the East Coast of the United States harshly criticized this legal framing because they viewed the unions as defending the interests of the employers and renouncing their solidarity with other groups of maritime workers.[16]

Spanish seafarers took leading roles in labor organizing in Cuba. In March 1901, the US occupation government approved a series of rules, previously agreed on by the longshoremen's and boatmen's guilds and representatives of the shipping companies, that regulated loading and unloading operations in Havana Bay as well as the salaries of the operators. A few years later, the shipping companies Ward Line, Munson Steamship Line, and Morgan Line breached the agreement, which caused socialist leaders to call for a general strike in the summer of 1904, the first major port strike in Cuba.[17]

There were many anarchists among the Spanish maritime workers. One was Juan Martínez de la Graña. Born in 1873 in Ferrol, he migrated to Cuba in 1905. He only stayed for a few years, working as a fireman before traveling to the United States in 1908. Many Spaniards joined the anarchist movement after migrating, without having participated in it while in Spain. Martínez de la Graña, however, was an anarchist before migrating. He almost immediately connected upon his arrival in Cuba with the Galician biweekly anarchist newspaper *Germinal* and Havana's *¡Tierra!* He wrote articles describing Havana's social reality and the prospects for anarchist organizing. He also gave an anti-immigration speech, a position that many Spanish anarchists on the island shared.[18] Many Spanish anarchists who migrated to the Americas viewed immigration as a trap because migrants were unaware of the true socioeconomic reality of the countries they arrived in. The anarchists felt the need to warn potential migrants in Spain of the harsh working and living conditions they would surely encounter.

Spanish anarchists on the island organized independently and in unions, but socialist and reformist tendencies in the movement remained stronger and counted many influential Spaniards as proponents. Juan Martínez de la Graña expressed amazement that workers at the Herrera Shipping Company affiliated with the Liga Marítima, a business-led trade association.[19] In 1903, the Asociación de Profesionales Navales de Cuba (Association of Naval Professionals of Cuba) formed, integrating maritime workers and machinists. Two years later, in 1905, the Asociación de Maquinistas Navales (Association of Naval Machinists) was organized.[20]

Martínez de la Graña, alarmed by the reformist tendencies of stevedores at the Port of Havana, promoted in 1906 an anarchist-oriented firemen's resistance society ("true defender of the interests of our class").[21] In addition, he proposed an assembly of workers with an unequivocally horizontal structure that would not constrain members to narrow bounds of struggle, a clearly anarchist position and a jab at socialists, in a column in ¡Tierra! Martínez de la Graña's proposal found little traction among seafarers and dockworkers. While anarchists and anarchism had some currency among these workers, they remained on the margins.[22]

Cuban authorities threatened to deport Martínez de la Graña for his labor organizing, and his disappointment at the headwinds he faced building a new group led him to leave Cuba. In May 1908, he took the steamer Havana to New York City. Martínez de la Graña maintained close relationships with comrades on the island after his departure. He published several articles in ¡Tierra! in which he analyzed the evolution of US maritime unionism, US society and politics, and anarchist organizing. He also closely followed conflicts at Cuban ports and occasionally returned. One occasion years later, on a trip to Havana in 1917, he assessed the possibilities of organizing sailors and firemen under syndicalist principles.[23]

A few years after Martínez de la Graña first left Havana in 1908, another Galician migrant arrived in Cuba who became a key element in organizing Havana port workers and other

workers on the island. Juan Arévalo Vieites believed unequivocally in social democratic reformism. Arévalo, born in Oleiros (A
Coruña) in April 1891, had migrated to Argentina with his family
in 1898. He worked at the Port of Buenos Aires in cold storage,
where he participated in the 1904 strike at just thirteen years
old. In 1905, Argentinian authorities deported him under the
Ley de Residencia back to Galicia, where he lived before traveling to Cuba in 1911. He settled in Gibara, Holguín, on Cuba's
southeast coast, working as a carpenter's assistant at the Santa
Lucía sugar mill. Police arrested him during a strike by workers
at the plant. After his release at the end of 1911, he moved to
Havana, where he began working as a riverside carpenter at
Sobrinos de Herrera y Compañía.

Havana's longshoremen went on strike in spring 1912,
and Arévalo and Ramón León Rentería assumed leadership
roles for workers at the Herrera company. Both men continued as important reformist leaders in Cuba's labor movement
into the 1940s. This conflict was part of a larger strike wave
throughout the Atlantic Americas. Juan Martínez de la Graña,
who also went by Xan da Graña, reconnected with maritime
workers in Havana and harshly criticized their leaders' reformism. He used the pages of *Cultura Obrera*, the newspaper of
the Unión de Fogoneros del Atlántico, to attack the strike resolution because it gave "companies fifteen days to solve the
conflict," which he likened to giving them "weapons to defend
themselves." Above all, his criticism focused on the agreement
including interests that had nothing to do with those of workers. "[Longshoremen lost] this movement by letting individuals who have no ideas, other than attending, take care of their
affairs on the eve of elections"[24]

Martínez de la Graña supported a radical model promoted
by firemen, "who declared themselves in solidarity strike with
them [and] are still firm in their struggle," based on a true class
spirit, but in opposition to the bureaucratic, hierarchical union
model contaminated by electoral politics.[25] *¡Tierra!* published

articles supporting Martínez de la Graña's position, one expression of a fight for organizational control, or at least the hearts, of Havana maritime workers.

In the same polemic in *¡Tierra!* Cuban anarchists openly disagreed with the resolution of the conflict, declaring, "The strike was proposed by dock and bay workers because of abuses that the shipping companies have been carrying out on a daily basis with their employees. . . . If this was the motive of the movement, [addressing] a circumstance that has not yet disappeared [and with] nothing . . . resolved in its favor, how can this movement be rationally ended?"[26] While most of Cuba's maritime workers affiliated with reformist-oriented unions, firemen favored anarchism. The Unión de Fogoneros, Marineros y Similares (Union of Firemen, Sailors, and Associates) began a strike on May 5 that drew support from the cart drivers' union by the middle of the month, which marked the worsening of the labor conflict. A statement from its executive committee, dated May 14, alluded to the "class spirit" and the "duty of solidarity" among all the "slaves of Capital," as well as avoiding "deadly prejudices of race, nationality or occupation" with the aim of "assaulting . . . the last stronghold of social unrest."[27] The Unión de Fogoneros seems to have dissolved soon after.

A new organization with the same name formed in 1915, with Juan Arévalo holding the position of General Secretary. Another Spanish anarchist migrant, Manuel Martínez Pérez, also participated in the group's activities. Martínez closely linked his organizing trajectory in Cuba to the defense of rational education. He served as president of the Agrupación Galaica Pro Instrucción Racionalista (Galician Pro-Rational Instruction Group) "13 de Octubre," founded in December 1913. In the union sphere, his work was much more controversial. He was expelled from the Unión de Fogoneros in December 1916, accused of having used the union for his personal benefit. Three years later, in December 1919, *La Voz del Obrero* attacked him, accusing him of being a police informer. He eventually returned to Vigo, Spain, in 1929.

Apparently, Martínez organized a rally in Havana in 1913 on the fourth anniversary of the assassination of Francisco Ferrer i Guardia, attended by representatives of a large number of the Galician immigrant education associations, usually grouped by their localities of origin.

During this period of organizing, Arévalo maintained a radical workerist perspective and used Marxist phrasing. The Unión de Fogoneros functioned as a platform in which different ideological tendencies coexisted. In 1914, Arévalo strongly supported the protest of Mexican workers against the US occupation of Veracruz during the Mexican Revolution and filed an official complaint with the American Federation of Labor. Shortly after, in 1916, Cuban authorities indicted and imprisoned him for sabotage. After his release at the end of 1916, he enlisted in the Cuban Navy as a ship's carpenter. In January 1919 he participated in a dockworkers' strike at the Port of Santiago de Cuba in military uniform. The strike grew into a general strike in that southern city, and Arévalo was court-martialed, sentenced to six months in prison, and expelled from the navy.

During these years, a serious economic crisis shaped organizing and politics in Cuba. Arévalo's approach to trade union reformism became less associated with a vague Marxism and more framed by traditional social democratic ideals. He explained his shift in view years later in newspaper articles in which he assessed his prior organizing, explaining that the reality of the island's historical moment forced him to change his views to advance what he called "constructive work" to achieve concrete improvements.[28]

Economic conditions in Cuba after World War I contributed to an increase in militancy among Cuban workers, although for many of them the times were already hard even before the postwar recession. The war had already caused, for instance, the end of manufactured tobacco exports, the closure of many tobacco factories, and unemployment for thousands of workers. Those that kept their jobs also faced difficult conditions. Inflation caused everyone to lose purchasing power. As the historian Louis Pérez summarizes this period, "The postwar depression transformed an already difficult situation into an impossible one."[29] Socioeconomic crisis did not strengthen the anarchist movement. Rather, it contributed to the deterioration of its influence, and reformist leaders consolidated their position.

Arévalo's political transition marked a turning point in maritime organizing. Despite the activism shown between 1914 and 1916, Arévalo soundly rejected the possibility of Union de Fogoneros's inclusion in the Industrial Workers of the World (IWW) and, consequently, the hypothetical convergence of maritime workers in Cuba and on the East Coast of the United States, unequivocally aligned with revolutionary syndicalist principles. By 1917, Arévalo established solid contacts with the AFL and formed a personal relationship with AFL president Samuel Gompers. Arévalo's position regarding the IWW generated controversy in the membership of the Union de Fogoneros that surfaced in the pages of *Cultura Obrera* in New York. Arévalo sent a letter to the newspaper in May 1917 criticizing what he interpreted as intrusion by outside anarcho-syndicalists in the internal affairs of Cuba.[30] He also alluded to an organizing visit made by Juan Martínez de la Graña to Cuba, taking advantage of his absence from Havana. In the letter, Arévalo explained that Cuba's maritime workers were not interested in the IWW project and that, on the contrary, they were working with the AFL to promote the Pan-American Federation of Labor.

The background of this proposal arose from the Pan-American Financial Congress of 1915, after which Samuel Gompers proposed that a Pan-American labor convention should be held to consider the problems resulting from the dangers of combined financial "interests that are already ready to help each other." Gompers proposed establishing a trade union structure in which reformist trade unions from across the Americas would join forces against radicals. The reformist, conservative craft union leadership viewed the IWW as a symptom of the disorder of the American industrial structure, while representing "all the hated characteristics of Bolshevism."[31] Gompers's organizational proposal was concretized at the founding congress of the Pan-American Federation of Labor in Laredo, Texas, in November 1918. The organization held four more congresses between 1919 and 1927 in New York, Mexico, and Washington.

During the founding assembly of the Federación Obrera de la Habana (Workers' Federation of Havana) in 1918, delegates debated two major questions: how to deal with the increase in the cost of living and whether they would send delegates to the congress of the Pan-American Federation of Labor. The delegates unanimously agreed to demand that the Cuban government undertake urgent actions to mitigate rampant inflation. The group took much longer to debate sending delegates to the congress, which had a strong anticommunist orientation. Arévalo emerged as the leading proponent for sending delegates. He faced strong opposition from the anarcho-syndicalists in the federation, and the measure was eventually defeated.

The Federación de Trabajadores de la Bahía de la Habana (Workers' Federation of the Havana Bay) became the most important maritime organization in this period. It was founded in 1918 with a reformist orientation and led by Arévalo. According to Robert Alexander, in September 1918 it included fifty-four hundred organized dockworkers.[32] In March 1919, Arévalo led a strike by port workers demanding a wage increase to offset their loss of purchasing power due to continued economic problems. His reformism and moderation did not endear him to Cuban authorities, who again arrested and imprisoned him. A few weeks after his release in April, he participated in the founding of a new organization that grew to great importance in the labor movement of Havana, the Federación de Obrera de la Bahía (Workers' Federation of the Bay). This new federation formed with the aim of integrating all the port workers of the bay.

In 1929, when taking stock of the trajectory of Cuba's labor movement in the first third of the twentieth century, Arévalo referred to the importance of the economic crisis and said that the trade union movement remained active: "We can calculate that, despite the economic crisis we endure, the labor shortage, and everything that can be deduced from this painful economic situation, there are more than two hundred thousand organized workers."[33] He also wrote that a definitive break between anarcho-syndicalists and reformists occurred in 1920 due to government repression and the failure of strikes. He criticized the tactical mistakes of anarchists for their overreliance on the general strike and their refusal to negotiate social and economic improvements. Spanish socialist organizations, both the Unión General de Trabajadores (General Workers' Union, UGT) and the Partido Socialista Obrero Español (Spanish Socialist Workers' Party, PSOE) as well as broader currents of social reformism influenced these shifts in Cuba.[34] As a result, reformism emerged victorious in Cuba, both in ideological currents and in trade union organizing, but, as if it were an obligatory toll, reformism could not overcome the widespread anti-American feeling that permeated the Cuban labor movement.

Despite the clear acceptance of reformism by the labor movement, at the end of 1919 a US diplomatic report implicated the "anarchist Juan Arévalo" in distributing propaganda about the Russian Revolution in Cuba through his supposed contacts with anarchists in New York, New Jersey, Massachusetts, and Los Angeles.[35] Given Arévalo's political positions, it is clear he fought against anarchists in Cuba rather than being an anarchist himself. This information might simply be incorrect, as government reports during the First Red Scare in the United States often were. It could have been a settling of scores against Arévalo for failing to bring the Maritime Federation of the Havana Bay under AFL control or influence. Most probably it is evidence of the strong repressive turn by the US government against all actors that could be perceived as radicals or sympathizers. The historian Josef Opatrný argues that naming Arévalo as an anarchist in the cable was unquestionably incorrect because both Arévalo and the other reformist leaders held an openly critical position toward the Soviet revolution, usually expressed from the newspapers *El Socialista* and *Acción Socialista*.[36]

By 1920, workers at the Port of Havana clearly identified with reformist leadership. The government of Alfredo Zayas, in power between 1921 and 1925, legalized their unions and established a tripartite agreement involving the union, port authority, and government representation that served as an instrument of labor mediation when conflict boiled in the docks. Anarchists, who still represented a substantial number of dockworkers, strongly opposed these agreements but could not prevent their implementation, and the reformist drift fulfilled its intended objectives. Reformists like Arévalo worked to advance their view of social democracy from the union base into Cuban politics in a similar fashion as the Partido Socialista Obrero Español (Socialist Workers Party of Spain). The founding of Cuba's Partido Radical Socialista (Radical Socialist Party, PRS) in 1920 followed this approach. The PRS was a social democratic and non-Marxist group that promoted political negotiation for social reforms in the labor sphere.[37] PRS proposals resulted in pioneering legislation for the eight-hour workday for government employees, the limitation of working hours in shops, the prohibition of work for children under fourteen, and the Ley de Accidentes Industriales (Law on Industrial Accidents).

Arévalo edited the newspaper *La Unión del Marino*, a monthly organ of the Unión de Fogoneros, and in 1921 he founded the weekly *Acción Socialista*, which became the unofficial organ of the Socialist Party.[38] Other reformist leaders in Cuba included Francisco Doménech and Luis Fabregat. Both served as secretaries of the Partido Radical Socialista and as reformist labor leaders in the Federación Obrera Nacional.

Juan Arévalo in 1929

Source: *Revista Cosmópolis*, Madrid, September 1929. Hemeroteca Digital, Biblioteca Nacional de España (Digital Newspaper Archive, National Library of Spain).

By 1925, Arévalo's situation had radically changed. He left the Federación Obrera de la Bahía while facing accusations that he had misappropriated funds. He joined the Hermandad Ferroviaria (Railway Brotherhood) shortly after—surprisingly, as his background was in maritime work. He represented the Havana area in the union in 1926 and rose to the position of secretary. Arévalo's view toward anarchism remained consistent. He declared, "The Hermandad Ferroviaria will never be radical. The transport organization must necessarily be conservative." However, this "yellow" position did not prevent him from being expelled from the union in 1928, along with other reformist leaders, accused of boycotting a strike being carried out by the railway train drivers.[39]

The Hermandad Ferroviaria divided into two antagonistic factions. A minority group of communists pushed against a reformist majority led by Arévalo and Otero Busch, who believed in working with the government and arbitration as an instrument to resolve labor disputes. Both leaders, despite the communist group's strong opposition, promoted the union's incorporation into the Pan-American Federation of Labor, which now included the Confederación Regional Obrera Mexicana (Regional Federation of Mexican Workers, CROM) and, of course, the American Federation of Labor, both strongly anti-communist organizations. In 1925, the Hermandad Ferroviaria and the Federación Marítima, along with other smaller trade union organizations, formed the Federación Cubana del Trabajo (Cuban Federation of Labor), led by the social democratic leader Luís Fabregat.

In 1925, Gerardo Machado was elected president of the Republic of Cuba. He would remain in power until a military coup in August 1933. Between 1925 and 1928, his government focused attention on developing important public works and limited social reforms. His economic program tried to reconcile the interests of the different sectors of the Cuban bourgeoisie and American capital, offering stability to the middle class and new jobs to the working class, all combined with a selective but fierce repression against political adversaries and opposition movements. He forced modifications to the constitution in 1927 to facilitate his re-election, after which his regime became increasingly repressive.

Arévalo attributed Machado's electoral victory to "his political campaign" making "great promises" for "improvement and, especially, for the working class." Based on these promises, some of the reformist leaders, like himself, supported Machado's campaign.[40] This close relationship with the Machado dictatorship was the most controversial facet of Arévalo's trade union and political career. In the middle of the dictatorship, Arévalo showed unflinching support for Machado and shamelessly praised the "successes" of the dictatorship in labor matters: "We believe it a duty to declare that, in spite of what is said about alleged tyranny existing, our organizations have not found obstacles, and the same honorable President of the Republic, General Machado, has been inspiring many laws of a social nature, such as retirement. . . . President Machado has begun by granting us participation in the governing bodies . . . and has reiterated his firm intention to provide our class with comprehensive legislation protecting labor, women, children, and the elderly."[41]

Arévalo, who was a freemason like Machado and belonged to the lodge "Hiram no. 34" of the Gran Oriente Nacional of Cuba, was publicly accused not only of having actively collaborated with "Machadismo" but also of being equally responsible for the repression unleashed by the regime. Caught in this contradiction between defending the principles of justice and freedom and exhibiting a more than questionable political performance, Arévalo reacted with the publication of an exhaustive document in which he tried to justify his public activity in that infamous period. The report argued that when the Hermandad Ferroviaria proposed a general strike in March 1930, Machado threatened to outlaw and suppress the strike promoters and, in that moment, when all the country was on the side of the president and no one dared to face it, the only exception had been the Hermandad Ferroviaria. In his reading of the facts, faced with the dilemma between loyalty to the president and loyalty to the union, he chose the union.[42]

Police arrested Arévalo along with the organization's central committee as a result of the strike and imprisoned them.[43] After Arévalo's release, he continued to maintain an active militancy in the committee, in addition to being a delegate of the Federación de Trabajadores de la Madera (Federation of Woodworkers), the Federación Marítima, and other positions. He claimed that until Machado's ouster in 1933, the reformist movement sought to remain strictly within the law, in an apolitical position, to obtain legislative improvements along with the release of imprisoned workers. Nevertheless, and despite his self-exculpation, Arévalo's position aroused much criticism and explicit accusations of opportunism. Some writers such as Carleton Beals, who wrote shortly after Machado's fall, describe the Federación de Trabajadores as a "puppet organization of Machado" and point out that Arévalo had published photographs of the former president with captions such as "the true friend of labor" in the newspaper *Acción Socialista*. Beals also describes a confrontation between Arévalo and Fabregat during the split of the Cuban Federation of Labor in 1930. Beals attributes this dispute to the leaders' rivalry to get the approval of President Machado.[44]

In this confrontation, Arévalo accused Fabregat of being paid by the police, and, in response, Fabregat published manifestos and pamphlets with photographs of alleged letters sent by Arévalo to the police in which appeared lists of "radical" workers who were to be expelled or arrested.[45]

After the overthrow of Machado in August 1933, police arrested Arévalo and imprisoned him in Havana's fortress of La Cabaña. After release he traveled to New York and from there onward to Galicia, only to return to Cuba in 1936. On the island he rejoined the maritime sector and participated in the creation of the Federación Nacional de Trabajadores Marítimos

(National Maritime Workers' Federation) and served as its first organizing secretary. He helped found the Confederación de Trabajadores de Cuba (CTC) and served as its secretary of foreign affairs and later as deputy director of the organization's magazine, which emerged in 1939. During this later period of his life, Arévalo continued to follow the reformist outlook, and leaders close to him faced accusations of corruption. There are indications that, shortly before being shot and killed by several gunmen on September 1, 1948, in Havana, he had traveled to Argentina and met with President Juan Perón.[46]

Conclusion

The AFL attempted to organize workers in Cuba, Puerto Rico, and the Panama Canal Zone. Samuel Gompers even traveled to Cuba during the tobacco workers' strike of February 1900, but his efforts were unsuccessful.[47] The spread of reformist tendencies among maritime workers is perhaps the most important legacy of this organizing. In Puerto Rico, another Spanish immigrant, Santiago Iglesias Pantín, left the anarchist movement to lead reformist trade union organizing, a trajectory similar to that of Arévalo in Cuba. Arévalo helped steer the Cuban labor movement away from anarcho-syndicalism.

Similar to Iglesias, Arévalo saw in the United States a model of democratic progress, and his political imagination was captivated by the ideals of freedom of speech, the press, and assembly. He also believed that American democracy improved the living conditions of workers.[48] It is appropriate to interpret the fervent "Americanization" and reformist "pan-Americanism" advanced by Arévalo in this context against the anarchist internationalism that had Havana as its core and extended out through the Caribbean and beyond through Spanish-language networks.

Arévalo stood for a deeply antiradical unionism that defined its socialism against the radicalism of anarchist or communist positions, and he also maintained close ties with Cuban economic and political elites. Arévalo's cooperation with the Machado dictatorship, even with periodic contradictions, shows the importance of his role in controlling the militancy of workers led by anarchists and in guaranteeing the use of state power to protect US economic interests during the Machado government's severe repression.

Cuban maritime unionism is distinct from the political and organizing currents in the Southern Cone, although Argentine unions made significant commitments to their own state. The influence of the internal structure of the Cuban maritime sector is important. The predominance of small shipping companies, the limitation of coastal routes, and the presence of fewer immigrant workers in the maritime community than in Argentina or the United States greatly limited the impact of radical ideological options, such as anarchism, in maritime labor organizing.

As we will see in the next chapter, workers who crewed the American ships sailing along the southeastern coast of the United States lived very different experiences, characterized by the presence of numerous distinct groups of immigrant workers and the incorporation of African American sailors and longshoremen. The North American Atlantic Coast witnessed the emergence of ethnic union models among Spanish maritime workers who, since the creation of resistance societies, embraced the principles of revolutionary unionism and became a fundamental part of the maritime organization project promoted by the IWW.

CHAPTER THREE

The North American Atlantic

Syndicalism, Race, and Maritime Unionism

The lives of Spanish immigrant maritime workers in the United States during the early-twentieth century shared commonalities with Spanish migrants in other countries in the Americas: difficult work requiring few qualifications, strong shipboard hierarchies, and frequent mobility. Spanish maritime workers in the United States lived near ports, most often as sojourning single men without families. They formed community at workplaces and in cafés, inns, and boardinghouses but lived more geographically segmented lives than those in Cuba or Buenos Aires. Other factors distinguished those sailing from or working at US ports from other locations to the south. The most significant difference Spanish maritime workers faced in the United States was their experience within the US racial order. This constrained their positions on ships to below-deck labor, most often as firemen, and strongly limited shoreside job options. It also impacted their labor organizing. Facing exclusion or neglect because of their racialization and job categorization by the "white"-led International Seamen's Union (ISU) made it necessary for them to build separate "ethnic" unions.

Many in the United States viewed Spain as an enemy after the battleship *Maine* exploded in Havana's harbor and many viewed Spain's Catholicism with suspicion. Negative views toward Spaniards often took on racial dimensions reinforced by linguistic differences. However, Spanish immigrant workers created their space to organize, occasionally interracially. The Spanish organizer Genaro Pazos wrote in 1913 during a strike at the Port of Boston, "Anglo-Saxons call themselves white, and foreigners call us black, but whites continue to occupy their posts while blacks abandon them to fight like men; let me be black and fight like a man."[1] Much to the chagrin of Spanish consular representatives, many of these workers valued class solidarity more strongly than other potential bases of community.[2]

Spanish organizing efforts resulted in the formation of the Unión de Fogoneros, Cabos y Engrasadores del Atlántico (Marine Firemen's, Watertenders', and Oilers' Union of the Atlantic) in 1902. From a slow beginning, the union took on new life toward the end of the decade through the efforts of a group of Spanish anarchists. The firemen initially affiliated with the ISU, an AFL affiliate, for strategic reasons, as they sought to increase their strength by joining with the larger craft unions. The firemen retained a large degree of autonomy after affiliation, which allowed it to continue its radical organizational work under the protection of a conservative craft union structure. The ISU also financed the anarchist newspaper *Cultura Obrera*. The Unión de Fogoneros achieved organizing victories but also suffered bitter defeats while affiliated with the ISU before it split from the craft union and integrated into the Industrial Workers of the World in April 1913.

This chapter traces the development of Spanish maritime workers in the context of larger Spanish immigration to the United States, before situating the rise of the Unión de Fogoneros within global syndicalism. What follows is a history of the Unión de Fogoneros in the Port of New York and its organizing impact.

Spanish immigrants and maritime workers

Between 1880 and 1920, 96,500 Spanish migrants arrived in the United States, almost 30,000 of them at the Port of New York. Most migrants from Spain were single men between fifteen and twenty-three years of age, primarily from Galicia, Asturias, and the Basque Country. Only 18 percent of migrants from Spain were women at this time. Some women migrated to reunite with family members who had made the journey earlier. Others were minor daughters without inheritances, daughters of unmarried parents, single women without marriage prospects in Spain, or otherwise economic migrants. The migration pushes were many, as life was difficult in Spain for working-class and middle-class women. In the United States, women worked in garment factories, on farms, and in family businesses. Women migrants played a crucial role in maintaining the formal and informal networks established in cultural clubs and their communities.[3]

Spanish maritime workers in the United States were men, largely distinct from the larger cohort of Spanish migrants in this period, and they grew from small numbers in the mid-nineteenth century. Impermanence through the mobility of their work and their strong community near ports, with few ties to Spanish migrants elsewhere in the United States, marked their lives. Few of these maritime workers had a credentialed "skill" in existing trade hierarchies, and few had previous union experience before migrating. Organizers and propagandists who spoke their languages—*castellano* (Castilian), Galego, and Catalan—and understood the experiences, political culture, and traditions of their migrant community facilitated labor organizing in the early-twentieth century.

According to data provided by the Spanish Bulletin of the Superior Council of Emigration, between the years 1900 and 1909, a total of 9,045 men from Spain declared their professions as sailors, porters, firemen, et cetera upon their arrival at the Port of New York.[4] The year 1911 saw the largest number of

Spanish firemen on the East Coast, at approximately twenty-six thousand; ten thousand to fifteen thousand of these workers made New York harbors their homes; and roughly 60 percent were Galician.[5] The *Coast Seamen's Journal* reported in July 1919 that the majority of the five thousand National Industry Union affiliates were Spanish firemen.[6]

The port system around New York had nearly 800 miles of coastline and 350 miles of port frontage. It included seven bays, the mouths of four great rivers, and four estuaries extending from Manhattan to Brooklyn and Staten Island and along the coast to Bayonne, Hoboken, Jersey City, and the Port of Newark. In the early years of the twentieth century, approximately three hundred thousand people worked in maritime operations related to commerce and naval traffic in occupations such as sailors, longshoremen, controllers, barge and tug crew, truckers, trainmen, shipyard workers, storekeepers, and customs agents. At the time, it was the largest port system in the United States. In 1914, when many of these operations had already been mechanized, between forty thousand and sixty thousand people still worked at the port.[7]

The years between the 1890s and World War I brought efforts to improve the working conditions of seafarers through legislation and labor organizing. Between 1892 and 1899, the International Seamen's Union organized sailors, and the US Congress passed measures that slightly improved work at sea. The Maguire Act of 1895 and the White Act of 1898 abolished corporal punishment of sailors and imprisonment for desertion. More substantial change came in 1915 with the passage of the Seamen's Act, which further codified limits to how sailors could be punished, regulated working hours on board, and mandated safety requirements. This act also required that at least 75 percent of sailors be able to speak the language of the officers, and on US-based vessels this meant English.[8] Shipowners challenged these requirements, and the legislative path to improve working conditions of sailors was long.

Official reports indicate the breadth of international and linguistic diversity on vessels in this period: "There are steam lines in which the crews below deck understand very little or no English. They speak a type of Spanish that is a combination of Spanish and Portuguese."[9] What the source identified was that almost all the firemen were Galician and spoke their language, Galego. Most migrants from Spain spoke very little English. Ship officers spoke English among other languages, and few understood Spanish or Galego. Difficulty communicating impacted life onboard vessels, especially for those below deck. It was not uncommon for shipping companies to sanction firemen for not complying with orders that they likely could not understand.[10] Clearly, language difficulties complicated the life of crew members on US ships by exacerbating vertical hierarchies of a ship's command structure.

Crew members also faced difficulties communicating with each other. Crewmen from Cuba, the Dominican Republic, Puerto Rico, Spain, Argentina, and other Spanish-speaking countries spoke a common language. Portuguese- and Italian-speaking workers could communicate with them, owing to the proximity of their languages and their own experiences over the course of their transnational working lives. Caribbean sailors speaking French or Creole had more difficulty, as did Anglophone and Greek crewmen. The lives of these maritime workers were polyglot, international, and marked by their movement.

The first organizing attempts in the United States by Spanish maritime workers began in the nineteenth century. The Spanish-language anarchist newspaper *Fuerza Consciente* later published an article looking back at the movement; author José M. Taracido dated its origins to 1870. In this account, a group of four Spanish sailors (almost certainly Galician) launched a propaganda campaign at the Port of New York to "make a sea workers' union to free us from the shipping exploitation of companies."[11] Scant historical records remain from these early organizing efforts. Galician anarcho-individualist Dionisio Freijomil later noted nascent organizing activities among Spanish maritime workers, especially firemen, in 1891: "Why do you not imitate us and those rebels who by '91 were on the ships, where you are?"[12]

In 1902, Spanish maritime workers in New York founded the Unión de Fogoneros, Cabos y Engrasadores del Atlántico. In the summer of that year the union promoted a strike among Spanish maritime workers at the Port of New York, but we lack concrete details. In October, the union requested incorporation, as an ethnic section, into the Marine Firemen's, Oilers', and Watertenders' Association of the Atlantic and Gulf, an organization affiliated with the International Seamen's Union in the largest US craft union, the American Federation of Labor. Between 1902 and 1907, union activity and membership seems to have been limited, and there is only evidence of a single Spanish-speaking union delegate, Frank Ernesto, during these years. In 1907, the ISU hired Fred Benson to organize African American, Italian, and Spanish sailors on the Atlantic Coast. The well-funded efforts found little success given the entrenched racism in the "white" union, but they were significant and fit within other multiracial and multilingual organizing pushed by vocal minorities in the AFL like the United Laborers organizing campaign in California.[13] The Spanish firemen were not swayed by the overture and did not join the union because Dan Sullivan remained an ISU leader and discriminated against immigrants.[14] However, the efforts may have softened the organizing ground for the ISU and created limited connections with Spanish sailors. According to the Spanish anarchist and union organizer Genaro Pazos, a few Spaniards served as delegates—for example, a fireman known as Tuerto (One-Eyed) Coruñés.[15]

The year 1909 brought new attempts to organize Spanish maritime workers by the ISU. Benson made a propaganda tour through Atlantic ports with two representatives of Britain's National Sailors' and Firemen's Union (NSFU).[16] The trio collaborated with a small group of Spanish-speaking maritime workers who included Argentinian José Berenguer, the Galicians Secundino Brage and Juan Martínez de la Graña, and the Catalan Jaime Vidal. Their efforts resulted in a greatly expanded Unión de Fogoneros. In 1910, these men were all founding members of the small anarchist collective Solidaridad Obrera (Worker Solidarity) that met at the Brooklyn Workers' Circle hall on Fulton Street and included firemen, sailors, and tobacco workers.[17] This group made two crucial decisions that shaped Spanish organizing at the port: they decided to channel their organizing efforts through the Unión de Fogoneros, and they decided to publish their own newspaper. The first issue of *Cultura Proletaria* rolled off the press in 1910; its name was changed to *Cultura Obrera* in 1911.

Solidaridad Obrera maintained a strong internationalist perspective and was possibly the successor to a group called Solidaridad Internacional (International Solidarity), established in New York in 1901, which seems to have only managed sporadic activities. Solidaridad Internacional was formed to assist workers participating in the general strike in the Galician city A Coruña, responding to a call for solidarity in the anarchist newspaper *La Revista Blanca*, published in Madrid at the time.[18] In the late-nineteenth and early-twentieth century, New York was one of the global hubs of anarchism, along with other crucial cities in the North America, including Tampa and Ybor City, Florida; Paterson, New Jersey; Los Angeles; and Havana.[19] Spanish anarchists fit into New York City's rich radical world. In 1909, the core Spanish anarchists in Solidaridad Obrera formed the New York Spanish Revolutionary Committee Constitution and published the "Manifiesto de los libertarios españoles en favor de la Revolución libertarian en España" (Manifesto of the Libertarian Spaniards in Favor of Libertarian Revolution in Spain). Jaime Vidal, who had recently fled Spain and arrived in the United States, signed the manifesto and became one of the most visible Spanish anarchists in America. This anarchist agitation showed little interest in labor organizing around bread-and-butter issues. Rather, it organized protests in New York City against the repression during Barcelona's Tragic Week uprising in 1909 and condemned Francisco Ferrer Guardia's murder by firing squad at Montjuïc Castle the same year.[20]

Organizing of Spanish maritime workers by the "white"-led ISU continued to face difficulties from multiple directions. Most Spanish workers had limited experience in trade unions, though most had sailed many thousands of kilometers and called in ports with strong radical traditions.[21] They also understood their racialized position on ships, in US society, and where they would stand in the ISU. Anarchist organizing at this point was not numerically significant, but dedicated organizers pushed forward and punched above their weight in their community. These key individuals, migrants from Spain themselves, and their groups published newspapers that spread their ideals, organized associations, and advanced specific union projects. They also maintained interpersonal connections with anarchists in Europe, the Americas, and beyond through letters and travel that made the anarchist movement a global community.

Andrew Furuseth publicly welcomed the Spanish firemen organized by anarchists into the ISU. Furuseth, a Norwegian immigrant and a racist stalwart of trade union organizing for white male workers, warmly thanked the new Spanish members for their moderation and understanding of trade union affairs. Spanish workers constituted 85 percent of all firemen working on the Atlantic Coast at the time. Furuseth's racist opposition to immigration and organizing positioned unions as a vehicle to protect the dominance of "white" workers, especially from Asian workers. He included the racial breadth of Spanish-speaking laborers in his racial categorization, yet organizing these workers in their trade did not threaten the position of "white" workers.[22]

Congressional testimony in 1911 by senior ISU leaders

including Furuseth, Marine Firemen's Union secretary general George Bodine, congressmen James Burke (Pennsylvania) and William Ewart Humphrey (Washington State), and labor leader William B. Wilson helps us understand their view toward Spanish firemen in the Atlantic:

> Burke: I would like to know the reason for the employment of such a large proportion of Spanish for firemen.
>
> Bodine: I think the only reason is that for some physical reason they make better firemen.
>
> Burke: Is it because they stand the heat better?
>
> Bodine: Well, it may be that. I think the other reason is that they are a more sober race than the Anglo-Saxon firemen. . . . I don't think there is any better firemen than the Anglo-Saxon; but it may be through liquor or some other reason that he doesn't stand the strain like the Spanish.
>
> Humphrey: Does the question of wages enter into it?
>
> Bodine: Spanish, to-day, get just as high wages as the Anglo-Saxon.
>
> Furuseth: Did they originally?
>
> Bodine: Not originally; no. Before they were organized the Spaniards received lower wages for their work.
>
> Wilson: I notice that the total number of Spanish employees or crew on vessels—that they have 26,059 out of a total number of members of crews of 192,191.

Bodine: Is that the whole country or just the Atlantic coast alone?

Wilson: The United States.

Bodine: I was speaking on the Atlantic—80 per cent of the firemen.

Wilson: You are speaking only of firemen?

Bodine: I was only speaking of the firemen when I made that statement that I thought 80 per cent of the firemen on the Atlantic were Spaniards.[23]

The Spanish sailor Manuel Bugueiro aptly expressed a view from the other direction in *Cultura Proletaria*: "Let us teach once and for all that if Spanish blood completes physical labor, it also serves to emancipate itself from being carried and brought as if it belonged to people without culture. Let's show that we're worth something more since we're crewing all three parts of U.S. shipping."[24] Spanish anarchists understood the position of the ISU leadership toward themselves and the workers with whom they organized and viewed their cooperation as tactical. Juan Martínez de la Graña later wrote in 1913, "There are many means of propaganda for ideas, and, regardless, I am convinced that if we want our ideals to make their way among the great mass, it is up to us anarchists to introduce ourselves into workers' societies, however conservative they may be, to make propaganda in them."[25]

The Spanish anarchists knew the craft union model from Spain, but it did not reach deeply into the working class. The first maritime trade union in Spain, the Asociación de Maquinistas Navales (Association of Naval Machinists), formed in 1878 and was concentrated in Barcelona and Bilbao. Officers organized early maritime unions in Spain, exclusive to their ranks.[26]

Between 1890 and 1920, trade unions at Spanish ports had few members and continued to largely exclude unskilled workers, sailors, and firemen. Meanwhile the large federations in Spain like the anarcho-syndicalist Confederación Nacional del Trabajo (CNT) and the socialist Unión General de Trabajadores (UGT) expanded slowly to include maritime labor.[27]

Given this distinctly mixed and challenging background in Spain and across the Atlantic, Spanish anarchist organizers seemed to take advantage of the trade affiliations of workers in their organizing through their shared job roles on board.[28] Spanish organizers in North America took a pragmatic approach, added members, and collaborated with unions affiliated with the AFL in a similar way as those in South America. All the while, they maintained important connections with anarchists throughout the Americas and Europe.[29] Spanish anarchists exercised a form of pragmatism while not renouncing their core beliefs in the general strike, industrial unions, the autonomy of local sections, and rejection of electoral politics. Further, their incorporation into the AFL challenged its conservatism and racism. In fact, grassroots organizers often pushed against the dominant forces in the AFL through more inclusive organizing.[30] That they did not win the day should not obscure them from historical memory.

Additionally, the ISU could be useful to anarchists. The federated structure of the AFL and ISU offered a degree of independence for locals. It also provided trade union protections to firemen who joined and space to continue to spread syndicalist ideals among maritime workers. Jaime Vidal explained that integration into the AFL expanded the network of solidarity for maritime unions in labor conflicts and provided an ideological platform to promote "more radical and modern" methods in those organizations.[31] If the ISU could help workers win salary increases and other immediately tangible benefits as the radicals continued to promote rational schools, finance propaganda, and solidarity, then it made good sense to use these advantages.[32]

Revolutionary syndicalism and the Unión de Fogoneros

"Revolutionary syndicalism" describes movements defined by direct action, heirs of the federalist and antipolitical faction in the First International. Anarcho-syndicalism or anarchist syndicalism was a radical tendency operating in similar terrain, but the largest syndicalist unions in the late-nineteenth and early-twentieth centuries omitted "anarchist" from their names. It is a far more productive endeavor, however, to document how historically situated movements articulated their ideals and how they organized in conversation with ideologies or political programs. The French Confédération Général du Travail (General Confederation of Labor, CGT) advanced syndicalism as an organizational form after its formation in 1895. In Italy a current broke from the Italian Socialist Party in 1912 to form an autonomous union organization, the Unione Sindacale Italiana (Italian Syndicalist Union, USI), which identified itself within the revolutionary syndicalist tradition. In Argentina, rival movements clearly differentiated between anarchism and syndicalism and struggled for influence over the labor movement. The Federación Obrera Regional Argentina (Argentine Regional Labor Federation, FORA) rejected the anarcho-syndicalist label because it considered itself a purely anarchist organization.[33] In the United States, an amalgam of interests including discontented trade unionists, socialists, and anarchists founded the Industrial Workers of the World in 1905. Through organizational and ideological consolidation, it soon became the most important syndicalist organization in the United States. It positioned the general strike and direct action as key to revolutionary change.[34]

The French radical Amédée Dunois defended revolutionary syndicalism as the highest phase of anarchism at the 1907 International Anarchist Congress in Amsterdam. He argued that syndicalism and antimilitarism elevated anarchism from theory to practice. In Dunois's view, anarchism could be transformed into a concrete program for social change through revolutionary syndicalism: "We see [in syndicalism] the most finished theoretical expression of different proletarian tendencies."[35] Pierre Monatte also defended the need to create revolutionary unions at that congress. For Monatte, revolutionary syndicalism entailed non-participation in politics, and, like the IWW, he viewed direct action as crucial to working-class emancipation.[36]

Historians Marcel Van der Linden and Wayne Thorpe describe revolutionary syndicalism as a movement and ideology that combined the struggle for immediate improvements with the drive to construct a new society through direct action. This program rejected political means like elections, not politics more broadly, in the pursuit of ends such as the abolition of capitalist system and the establishment of a society organized by associations of producers. Revolutionary syndicalism appealed to anarchists in that it did not aspire to dissolve individuals into a large political body; rather, it aimed to free individuals from these forms of control.[37]

Two Catalan anarchists were leading proponents and organizers in this tradition on the Atlantic Coast and beyond. Jaime Vidal was a leading proponent of syndicalism among Spanish-speaking workers on the East Coast of the United States. Between 1909 and 1911, this former collaborator of Francisco Ferrer i Guàrdia dedicated himself to weaving together a network of immigrant workers from the Iberian Peninsula in the New York area. Pedro Esteve was an even brighter light who spread the word through the newspapers *Cultura Proletaria* and *Cultura Obrera*, in speeches, correspondence, and collaborations with Italian anarchists.[38] Esteve, strongly influenced by Kropotkin's thought and a firm defender of organizations, supported the use of revolutionary violence and tirelessly wrote and agitated after he returned to New York from Florida in the autumn of 1911.[39]

The Unión de Fogoneros based its organizing around syndicalist principles, and its history is interwoven with its leading organizers like Vidal, Esteve, and others. Labor below deck, feeding the furnaces of American ships, bound together its members.[40] The union spread its ideals through articles and editorials in *Cultura Obrera* that took the form of a serialized programmatic booklet for long-term readers. While not all seamen could read, these ideas permeated discussions, and groups often read newspapers aloud. Maritime workers formed a diffuse network connected by mobile agitators transiting from port to port and ship to ship across a wide geographic space. *Cultura Obrera* integrated nodes by connecting dispersed and mobile workers through its role as an educational platform and coordination tool. Further, *Cultura Obrera* functioned as a big tent under which a large degree of difference among radicals existed. People sent messages, distributed slogans, attacked opponents, received complaints and criticism, transmitted ideology, extended solidarity, and otherwise engaged in the struggles of maritime workers in its pages.[41]

The Unión de Fogoneros maintained a stable presence in several Atlantic ports, with its strongest base in New York. From their headquarters in Brooklyn, both *Cultura Proletaria* and *Cultura Obrera* spread their organizing message and fought against the shipping companies.[42] Union leaders gave life to the transnational message behind the union's founding from New York. They turned the Port of New York into the nucleus from which the union organized in other Atlantic and Gulf ports and into Central and South America. *Cultura Obrera* exerted significant influence in the Spanish-language anarchist and syndicalist movement in North America, especially on the East Coast of the United States. The Partido Liberal Mexicano's newspaper *Regeneración*, published in Los Angeles, stood as the other most influential Spanish-language anarchist newspaper published in the United States during this period. *Cultura Obrera* organized solidarity and fund-raising campaigns to support fellow workers such as Cuban fireman Alejandro Aldamas and political prisoners in Spain and to finance the paper's continued publication. The publishers also used its pages to coordinate strikes and mobilizations in American ports and to support fellow workers in Havana, Tampico, and Buenos Aires.

Organizers for the Unión de Fogoneros understood the novelty of their position as anarchists within a craft union structure. They publicly congratulated each other for getting the conservative AFL to publish an openly revolutionary syndicalist newspaper yet did not restrict their revolutionary ambitions to a simple position of economic struggle. Rather, they understood, as Vidal reflected, that this impulse would have to be complemented by social struggle to produce truly profound transformations in society: "Workers' struggle alone, in spite of its advantages, for now would be useless and would prevent the producer from emancipating himself, just as the social struggle, separated from workers' struggle, would always lack the strength of the producing masses and would delay the accomplishment of emancipating principles."[43] Vidal also emphasized two concepts that were vital to those who longed for social transformation: union control over the workplace and unity between the different maritime trades to build the radical movement.[44] In their view of the process of liberation, autonomy was a fundamental value both for individuals and organizations. The Unión de Fogoneros opposed establishing centralized structures that would usurp the role of local assemblies and the possibility of concentrating decisions in the hands of a small group of leaders, acting outside of local control.

They also disdained political activity. They rejected instruments of political participation in liberal democratic systems, including political parties. For example, Unión de Fogoneros organizer Genaro Pazos urged his colleagues not to vote. Rather, they should pour their energy into organizing industrially and destroy the existing regime through the general strike for the "emergence of a society of Love, Freedom and Reason."[45] The Unión de Fogoneros developed an ethics of direct action that held that workers should not be governed; they must emancipate themselves. Leaders should not be recognized as such but rather as equals who contribute through their activism.[46] Workers may use direct action and even revolutionary violence as a defensive tool. Esteve wrote about violence as a mechanism of reaction, and many union members shared this view but with restraint. This came to bear in labor conflicts that turned into litmus tests for the union. Although strikes took place in climates of acute tension stoked by violent harassment by police and private security forces, only a small number of "conscious" militants responded violently. Few sailors and firemen engaged in such tactics.

Esteve used cryptic language in the editorial "The Only Way" (*El únicocamino)*, an appeal for the frontal resistance of maritime workers that concealed the implicit impossibility of its effectiveness in the current environment. Esteve explicitly defended the virtues of revolutionary syndicalism, direct action, and propaganda by the deed. He wrote, "There is no progress, there is no real advance, if it is not carried out in the deeds." But he urgently insisted, "We diminish as much as we can the strength of the authority [state], the profits of the capitalist, the faith of the priests. Let us be, in short, not the oil that greases but [rather] the corrosive that destroys. Without destruction no creation is possible. It is the fatal, inevitable law. From nothing, nothing can be done. Let us ruin [in order] to build."[47]

Its members organized the Unión de Fogoneros according to their horizontal and participatory values. "A craft organization cannot be a secret society and even less a monopolizing association."[48] They intentionally created rotating leadership positions, except that of a paid secretary without executive functions. The secretary acted more like a liaison between the different sections of the union and maintained relationships with the ISU. The union also financed delegates responsible for each port, elected by workers in local assemblies. Anti-organizational anarchists criticized such funding as being contrary to libertarian principles, and Argentine anarchists dismissed it as reformist.[49]

The union held regular meetings with rotating assembly presidents, although the membership usually elected as session presidents highly respected members who had moral standing. Thus, individuals such as Antonio Ucha, José Filgueira, Genaro Pazos, Pedro Esteve, Dionisio Freijomil, and Juan Martínez de la Graña all served as session presidents. The secretary, agents, and port delegates reported to the plenary at the assemblies, and discussions of financial matters followed. Attendance at meetings in 1911 and 1912 averaged between 150 to 200 members, reflecting the fact that many members might have been away aboard a ship.[50] Workers discussed a wide range of issues at the assemblies, including appointments of agents and delegates, contracting only with companies that recognized the union, applications for admission, expulsion of members associated with shipping companies, criteria for shipments, internal conflicts in union branches, and the need to ensure compliance with union rules.[51]

Jaime Vidal was a critical force in establishing a small cluster of social studies centers and libertarian libraries along East Coast port cities including in Jessup (Maryland), Brooklyn, White Plains, and Newark. These groups included firemen and maintained a stable trajectory for some years. Spanish anarchist migrants, along with other Spanish speakers, gave lectures, presented theatrical stage shows, organized poetry recitation groups, opened sociological libraries, taught English classes, and set up gyms. These groups also promoted the opening of libertarian tea rooms; such was the case with the grand opening of the New York Ferrer Tea and Lunch Room.[52]

Pedro Esteve's lectures served as the opening and closing of the Brooklyn Workers' Circle's cultural season, while the dances, almost always held in the Astoria Hall at 62 East Fourth Street in Manhattan, along with picnics, were the playful alternative to the "tainted" atmosphere of the Spanish cafés near the port. Spanish migrant anarchists dedicated themselves to promoting alternative cultural development in the Spanish community and established deep social ties throughout the North American anarchist movement through the common symbolic elements used in their organizing, such as those influenced by Catalan pedagogue Francisco Ferrer.

In 1910, Emma Goldman and Alexander Berkman convened anarchists in New York to establish the Francisco Ferrer Association during an event held at the Harlem Liberal Alliance, located on West 116th Street, in response to Ferrer's execution. The partnership stood behind the Ferrer Center and Modern School, which opened in St. Mark Square, Greenwich Village. Berkman, Harry Kelly, Leonard Abbott, and Jaime Vidal promoted the project. Vidal had been a close collaborator of Ferrer and served on the school's board of directors.[53] The Ferrer Center survived in its original location until 1914, when police repression and the loss of some financial support forced it to move to Stelton, New Jersey, where it remained active until 1953.

Newspapers bound together dispersed anarchist communities with interlocking linguistic, ideological, regional, and other characteristics. Solidaridad Obrera began publishing *Cultura Proletaria* in 1910, and this anarcho-syndicalist paper circulated among Spanish maritime workers on the Atlantic Coast. Juan Martínez de la Graña wrote in *Cultura Proletaria* in 1913 that Havana's *¡Tierra!* and Barcelona's *Tierra y Libertad* had circulated among Spanish-speaking sailors in 1907. Shipping companies and governments recognized the importance of these newspapers and targeted them. Repression by the Spanish government during Tragic Week and its judicial murder of Francisco Ferrer, however, increased the interest of Spanish workers in anarchism.

Spanish anarchist organizers also maintained utilitarian connections to the ISU and AFL that combined influence over hiring and drawing new members to the anarchist organization. Martínez de la Graña made clear in his 1913 article, "Although we did not sympathize with the International [Seamen's Union], it would be easy for us to leave it when we felt strong, as we left it in time."[54] Under the care of the omnipresent Jaime Vidal, *Cultura Proletaria* served as a loudspeaker for the organization of Spanish firemen. Vidal, Berenguer, and Brage consistently insisted on the need for Spaniards to join with the other "races" that were already walking the path of organization.[55]

An article in *Cultura Obrera* in 1912 articulated the way that many Spanish anarchists understood race. According to Lázaro García, a Spanish sailor living in New York, "There are no different races; only one, imperishable: the Human."[56] Such a resounding statement about the existence of a single human race was in line with universalist anarchist ideals about humanity and the defense of a sense of justice and equality. However, Spanish sailors entered the US racial order and formed their ideas of race in it. Racial categorization occurred both from the outside and from within, through all social and economic pathways. Most people, from the bosses to anarchists, viewed race through physical, geographical, and linguistic dimensions connected to both positive and negative attributes. Spanish maritime workers' understanding of race and their racialization through their entry into the deeply rooted racial order in the United States shaped their organizing efforts and worldviews.

The port world of bars, masculine culture, and place

In the port world, taverns and cafés rose to an almost mythical status for their socializing function. However, establishments that sold alcohol had a more sordid reality related to the economic exploitation and emotional control they could exercise over maritime workers. Many radicals and unionists viewed these locations as debased environments that distanced workers from their social and organizing potential. This view quickly becomes understandable if we consider that Spanish immigrants owned more than two hundred cafés, bars, and inns in the area surrounding the Manhattan and Brooklyn docks. The Spanish-speaking population of dockworkers never exceeded five thousand, which would make one drinking location for every twenty-five workers, though other area residents also patronized them. This pattern repeated itself in other Atlantic ports such as Norfolk, Boston, Philadelphia, and New Orleans but in smaller numbers.[57]

Thousands of Spanish sailors who passed through the port, waiting to embark on steamers, colliers, or tugboats that docked on the Hudson River or East River, used the saloons and *cafetines*, as the Spanish cafés in the New York port area were known, as places of residence and leisure. Workers celebrated ethnic holidays, consumed traditional meals, and drank *vino spagnolo* (Spanish wine).[58] Labor recruitment occurred in these locations, as did the sharing of news and information between laborers about work or their countries of origin or travels. Some tavern landlords served as intermediaries for their customers by cashing checks, offering loans, or lobbying local politicians.

The characteristics and the popularity of taverns and cafés catering to Spanish-speaking maritime workers in the United States reveal another vital function. Spanish migrants in the United States did not reach the numbers to develop broader community spaces like those in Cuba and Argentina. These sojourning, single, male, marginalized workers—marginalized both in occupational status and often by poor English skills that isolated them from broader society—constructed their strongest ethnic and language-centered social relationships in cafés rather than in other community institutions.

Tavern culture, with its often-rough competition and male camaraderie, played an important role in shaping the masculinity of workers, within which alcohol consumption was a central expression. Workers strengthened group ties through celebrations of meeting with old crewmates, the arrival of news from their families, a new shipment, and above all, receiving their pay. Sailors who did not drink ran the risk of exclusion from these supporting networks because workers viewed them as *aristo* (aristocratic) for thinking differently or more of themselves than of their peers. Spanish sailors and firemen completed hard physical labor with their hands and developed a masculine workplace culture that joined power and virility with craft pride. By spending their leisure time drinking in cafés, maritime workers participated in a dynamic, almost exclusively male community.

The personality and exploits of the Galician migrant Andrés Balsa exemplify the masculine focus of this community. Born in Mugardos in 1883, he trained in Greco-Roman wrestling during a stay in England while a professional boxer, before traveling to the United States in 1910 to put his pugilism skills to work in search of fast money. During the 1910s Balsa participated in dozens of heavyweight fights across the United States and always had the enthusiastic support of his compatriots. Toward the end of his fighting career, he fought against mythical heavyweight fighters such as the Argentine Luis Firpo and the American champion, the "Auburn Bulldog" Floyd Johnson, just before his fortieth birthday. Balsa returned to Spain in July 1920 with his fighting career in decline. After 1926 he dedicated himself to training a *fútbol* (soccer) team.[59]

Men frequented bars especially when they lacked other types of distractions away from work. Cafés and taverns provided a refuge for migrant maritime workers and a substitute for domestic life. Living and working in hostile environments, their need to combat loneliness and create spaces of trust and security prevailed over moral warnings of union leaders or possible objections against enriching café owners through their patronage. According to historian Jorge Uría, taverns had many functions. Imbibing was a given, but bars also hosted dances, singing, discussions, and debates. Mutual aid societies or clandestine societies may also have met on their premises, as they did in Italian anarchist circles in London.[60] Taverns functioned as one of the centers of popular culture for work-ers.[61] The historian Madelon Powers documents this kind of social function of cafés and port taverns. She emphasizes that, beyond drinking, these locales stimulated feelings of camara-derie, unity, and community among their customers, especially among the regulars.[62] Her studies document regular customers often sharing the same ethnicity or occupation and strength-ening their social bonds through the process of meeting and drinking together.

Historian Tom Goyens examines the role of bars among German immigrant anarchists in New York. Breweries owned by German immigrants dotted the cityscape of the Lower East Side. They sold lager and hot food, served as meeting places for assemblies and social activities, such as picnics and excursions, in addition to hosting activities of other immigrant groups. Despite the astonishing growth of industrial capitalism, the entanglement of business and politics, and the omnipresent presence of police power, German immigrant anarchists built autonomous spaces in bars that Goyens calls a "sphere of free action," in which they found support, created a base to grow their movement, and promoted the organization and education of non-anarchist migrants.[63]

The bars and cafés frequented by Spanish maritime work-ers functioned differently from the German beer halls in New York. Although the bars frequented by Spanish workers were ethnic businesses, they did not give rise to the social organizing to advance the interests of maritime laborers that the German beer halls did for anarchists in the city. Spanish anarchists and labor organizers viewed bars as sites of moral degradation, typ-ical of capitalism, in which violence, gambling, and alcoholism comingled. Emilio García wrote in *Cultura Obrera*, "So many of us, at the end of trip, go from café to café, playing, getting drunk, and also the daggers and guns shine."[64] Accusations of extortion, usury, and even pimping by café owners frequently appeared in the pages *Cultura Obrera*. Workers also criticized bar owners who acted as labor agents for shipowners, requiring that the unemployed pay high commissions for new contracts or lodge at their inns to gain work.

Like many of their European counterparts, Hispanic anarchists showed themselves to be implacable critics of what they viewed as bourgeois morality. In their attempt to eradicate social scourges such as alcoholism, anarchists often viewed work, sobriety, and sacrifice as fundamental working-class values. Pedro Esteve criticized what he viewed as the dependence of sailors and firemen on the bars and cafés. For Esteve, their propensity to visit cafés owned by other Spaniards, or to "throw a gray hair in the air" (purchase sex), were manifestations of the old and "defective" customs of their native villages. It was the continuation of a peasant mentality that prevented working-class men from enjoying a free life and education. Through his anarchist moralism, Esteve considered it incomprehensible that workers reveled in whiskey and other alcoholic beverages and frequently had violent exchanges among themselves, rather than taking advantage of the beauty and resources offered by North American cities.[65] This moralistic discourse is very present in the pages of *Cultura Obrera*. There are dozens of articles crying out against alcohol consumption and warning of its harmful effects, both morally and in purely economic terms. There is also much criticism of those who facilitated this escape, whether café owners or innkeepers. When some members defended the actions of bar owners in the newspaper's pages, the publisher responded forcefully: "Café owners should never be defended by unionists."[66]

Scholar Sara García de Orellán explains that class struggle is also "a struggle of emotional bodies in which political legitimacy is at stake," and this legitimacy is directly related to bodily health.[67] For this reason, spaces where people imbibe alcohol negatively impact political struggles because they work against the ideal of a healthy body pursued by both socialism and anarchism. Leading organizers like Esteve advocated for cafés to be replaced by societies based on "instruction, beauty and recreation" that would allow workers to learn the English language and adapt to "modern life."[68] Juan Martínez de la Graña viewed the situation differently. Although he was aware of the difficulties posed by bars for the expansion of social education and for their role in perpetuating vice and ignorance, he maintained a more pragmatic position. In Martínez's view it was better to reach agreements with owners to shut down their businesses on the days with trade union assemblies, to limit the sale of alcohol and gambling on card games, and, above all, to refrain from hiring Spanish immigrant women to attract patrons, which could lead to prostitution.[69]

Clearly then, the relationship between workers, anarchists, labor organizers, and café owners was layered in complexities. The innkeeper Gerardo Moscoso provides yet another view. In an exceptional decision, the Unión de Fogonero agreed to publicly boycott his inn. Through a statement of the "Press Committee," the union accused him of charging twenty dollars a month in exchange for "terrible food, a bed for two and deplorable hygiene."[70] The situation was complicated by the fact that occasionally this innkeeper organized fund-raising events for *Cultura Obrera*. The unionists criticized his lack of scruples in draining the resources of maritime workers through alcohol sales and using waitresses to attract patrons, possibly a front for prostitution.[71]

However, Moscoso also helped spread Unión de Fogoneros propaganda and appealed to sailors and firemen to avoid certain shippers to honor the agreements established between the union and shipping companies.[72] The relationship between the union leaders and the owners of the cafés and inns remained complex. Although publicly the union harshly attacked the role played by café owners, accusing them of being exploiters and agents of shipping companies, and of making money by controlling shipments, some owners, such as Moscoso, acted as allies of the union on certain occasions.

Beyond moral debates, contention over practical issues remained. If the café owners where many sailors and firemen boarded associated with shipping companies, it limited the union's ability to extend its power. "What I know, and no one can deny, is that when shippers existed, they did what they wanted to do with us. We had to pay a dollar for an inn and 75 cents in the café, embarking when they wanted and on the boat they wanted, and sometimes making us make a trip on each boat, having us then thirty or forty days ashore. The union freed us from these exploiters, [and] we embarked, in turn, and are free to go where we want, and we have imposed certain company conditions, and some still speak against the Union!"[73] This is why the union had to make efforts to attract café owners, despite their questionable social conduct and their reluctance to join the union.

Strikes: brief victories, bitter defeats

In the summer of 1911, port workers, railway workers, and sailors in Liverpool, England, walked off the job in what became known as "the great transport workers' strike." The conflict paralyzed the city and transformed unionism on the banks of the Mersey. Before the strike, workers organized in independent trade societies, whereas in this strike workers organized through inter-industrial solidarity, and all transportation unions acted jointly, which led to their victory.[74]

Workers and radicals in the Americas celebrated and took inspiration from this breadth of solidarity, particularly the Unión de Fogoneros, which organized along similar industrial lines. Articles in *Cultura Proletaria* invoked the need for solidarity among workers at this crucial moment and articulated their demands. In his regular section in the newspaper, "Movimiento Obrero Marítima" (Maritime Workers' Movement), Martínez de la Graña claimed, "The time has come for all seafarers to abandon the ships of those companies that do not accept the demands we have made. . . . Comrades, we have nothing to lose. We'll never be worse off than we are now."[75] The labor conflicts in Liverpool and New York opened the possibility of organizing a transnational network of maritime unions. Jaime Vidal wrote about an international federation of sailors that would integrate unions in China, Europe, Australia, and the United States.[76] The ISU, however, did not react with the same enthusiasm. It viewed the great strike through what it saw as the distinct and unreconcilable positions of the predominantly "white" long-shore workers and the mostly nonwhite immigrant sailors and firemen in Liverpool.

Maritime workers in New York viewed the events in England through the lens of their own strike, as part of a larger strug-gle between capital and labor. The Atlantic Coast Seamen's Union also called for strikes in the summer of 1911 at the Port of New York, both in solidarity with workers in Liverpool and to achieve local objectives. Workers targeted shipping compa-nies' routes between the Caribbean and Mexico.[77] The Unión de Fogoneros, affiliated with the ISU's Marine Firemen's, Oilers', and Watertenders' Union of the Atlantic and Gulf, attempted to win control of shipments, improve working conditions through agreements on rest, meals, et cetera, and increase salaries. Twenty thousand maritime workers participated.[78]

The striking workers formulated a broad platform that artic-ulated ways they wanted to improve their lives: "The demands are not solely for an increase in wages. The firemen say that they want to get out of the grip of the boarding-house masters. They allege that if they are not known to certain masters or do not live at certain boarding-houses, they are not able to obtain employ-ment."[79] On June 28, the shipping companies accepted the union demands. Strikers won the job action through their collective solidarity. The union began managing ship work assignments for Spanish sailors; innkeepers and café owners lost influence over hiring; and firemen saw their wages increase. One limitation was that the contract was annual and had to be renegotiated in the summer of 1912. Members of the Waterfront Federation formed through an alliance of three different unions: the Marine Cooks and Stewards Association of the Atlantic and Gulf; the Marine Firemen's, Oilers', and Watertender's Union of the Atlantic and Gulf; and the Atlantic Coast Seamen's Union. All three unions signed the agreement after a nine-day strike.

The Unión de Fogoneros contacted the anarchist group that published *¡Tierra!* to gain the support of Havana's longshore workers and sailors. Despite their efforts, those in New York did not receive the support they desired from Cuba. The Unión de Fogoneros had strong support in the Atlantic ports of New York, Philadelphia, New Orleans, and Norfolk, and that extended to Lake Michigan and the Pacific. Their affiliation with the International Seamen's Union helped prevent the recruitment of strikebreakers.[80] Juan Martínez de la Graña wrote of the strike, "Then came the fight, obtaining victory almost without any effort, and here we are propagating our ideals because we are not satisfied with what we have obtained, nor will we be even if they give us much more. We have gotten rid of the innkeepers, we have obtained more salaries, [and] the maritime companies had to accept recognition of the union."[81]

The 1911 strike increased the influence of the Unión de Fogoneros among maritime workers, and it sought to turn the Port of New York into a model for organizing in other North American Atlantic ports, the Caribbean, and Central and South America. An editorial in *Cultura Obrera* in February 1912 laid out its lofty goals by calling for the formation of a world transport federation to unify organizing across sectors and continents and to promote the declaration of a general strike.[82] They viewed industrial organizing and the general strike as vehicles for revolutionary change. Their organization had a much more limited reach, but the Spanish organizers' goals consistently transcended the local and national as they struggled to build a global union of maritime workers. They filled the pages of

Cultura Proletaria and *Cultura Obrera* with news of labor conflicts across the Americas, Europe, and Asia. Articles in their
newspapers also expressed their desire and efforts to establish common lines of action with firemen in Cuba, Argentina,
and Mexico.

This victory and new strength increased the number of workers who affiliated with the Marine Firemen's Union. By the end
of 1911 the union expanded to other Atlantic ports, including
Boston, Norfolk, and New Orleans, pushing the MFU's membership ranks to nearly ten thousand. The MFU secretary general
George Bodine sought to draw on this newly gained strength to
take control of the ISU. Bodine, a conservative trade unionist,
forged a tactical alliance with the radicals incorporated into the
MFU, including the Unión de Fogoneros.[83] In a quid pro quo,
Bodine pledged to withdraw ISU support for the La Follette Act,
which discriminated against the rights of foreign sailors. He
also supported transforming the ISU into an industrial union
without autonomous trade unions. In return, the Unión de
Fogoneros would support Bodine's effort to gain organizational
control. They intended to act at the ISU convention in Baltimore
in December 1911. Jaime Vidal and José Filgueira represented
the Unión de Fogoneros at the convention.[84]

The move against ISU leadership began by accusing Secretary
William Frazier of harboring racial prejudices against Spanish
workers and stressing that American delegates were not able to
attract maritime workers from southern Europe. While these
assertions may well have been based in fact, trade union racial
divisions reflected shipboard occupational segregation, making
their fight multilayered. African Americans (as well as other
people of African descent) and Spaniards worked as machinists and firemen below deck. African Americans also worked as
cooks, while "whites" worked almost exclusively as engineers
and officers. Trade unions reflected racial structures that limited
the occupations of people of color yet also reinforced these lines
within their own worker-controlled organizations. For example,

at the Baltimore convention, Oscar Carlson, the Philadelphia delegate of the Marine Firemen's Union, used the epithet "dagos" to refer to Latina/o workers.[85]

Bodine fulfilled his part of the alliance with the Unión de Fogoneros through his criticism of Senator Robert La Follette's maritime bill, but the alliance between Bodine and the Spanish workers failed to achieve its objective. Andrew Furuseth continued his control of the ISU thanks to his support base in the Pacific and Great Lakes. The white conservative trade unionist neither shared the radical impulses of the Spanish workers nor viewed them as equals in the union.

It would take more than a year for the official rupture between the Unión de Fogoneros and the ISU to occur, but the Unión de Fogoneros viewed the damage done by the failure of their attempt to transform the ISU from within as irreparable. It saw that its ideals of industrial unionism aligned with the Industrial Workers of the World and prepared to leave the ISU. The IWW, from its founding, spread through its songs and factored prominently into worker culture of the period. For example, one IWW song changed the name of the ISU to "I Sold You." Martínez de la Graña voiced another signal of the Unión de Fogoneros's discontent with the ISU in a March 1912 article that warned workers, "Today we see that this International is a bad stepmother, and in no way can we remain within it any longer."[86] Finally, two events precipitated the definitive rupture: the ISU refusal to continue financing *Cultura Obrera*, the far-reaching voice of the Unión de Fogoneros, and, above all, the failure of a strike in the summer of 1912. The lack of support for their newspaper was a clear signal of the ISU's lack of support for Spanish workers, but the failure of the strike proved even more concrete.

Shipping companies increasingly circumvented the 1911 agreement and regained many of their concessions before the agreement expired. As unions negotiated its extension in 1912, and despite the Marine Firemen's Union's efforts, the number of rival unions on the Atlantic Coast increased and had difficulty agreeing on a common platform. The New York seamen's unions—the International Longshoremen's Association (ILA), Atlantic Coast Seamen's Union, and International Seamen's Union of America—had joined the Waterfront Federation, an organization dominated by longshoremen. This organization called the strike in summer 1912, without ISU approval. The strike spread to all Transportation Workers Federation of America ports on the East Coast.[87]

On June 29, 1912, after months of preparation, thirty thousand workers walked off the job in Boston, Galveston, Hoboken, New Orleans, and New York. Jaime Vidal viewed the strike as being not only for a wage increase but also to organize and protect transport workers, whether sailor, longshoreman, fireman, coal passer, hoisting engineer, waiter, oiler, water tender, or checker.[88] Repression at the hands of police and the private security guards hired by the shipping companies increased tension at the docks. Violence occurred. In New York, police shot and killed the Galician worker Andrés Rodríguez from A Coruña. Police arrested Alejandro Aldamas, a fireman with Cuban roots, who stood accused of attacking a policeman and two representatives of the shipping lines. According to the *New York Herald*, Vidal, Esteve, his teenage daughter Violeta Esteve, and an Anglo-American named Milo Woolman led the strike.[89]

The strike faced difficulties from the start. The ISU-affiliated Marine Cooks and Stewards Union immediately crossed picket lines, and the separately organized engineers never considered striking. A few lines settled in the first week, and, although the firemen stood together, the participation of other sailors was spotty. Tens of thousands of longshoremen joined the strike at various points but fragmented into competing unions, each of which returned to work as they received concessions. When the ILA won a pay raise on July 29, ISU seamen quickly agreed to return to work, leaving the Spanish firemen isolated and with no alternative but to call off their strike.[90]

Defeat strongly impacted the unions that organized the strike, in terms of lost wages and morale. Unión de Fogoneros financial prospects looked dramatically different after it lost the strike. It closed its old headquarters and moved to Charlton Street near the Hudson River. Defeat also led to major internal dissension. The Unión de Fogoneros, which had achieved a great victory in 1911, withdrew from the ISU immediately after the failed strike in 1912 before joining the IWW in 1913.[91] In response, the ISU promoted a new organization into which the Atlantic Coast firemen could be integrated, entrusting organizing to former Marine Firemen's Union agent Oscar Carlson. The executive committee of the ISU adopted a statute in December 1913 reorganizing the firemen by granting a charter to the Marine Firemen's, Oilers', and Watertenders' Union of the Atlantic and Gulf in December 1913.[92] This change was less about attracting the Spanish firemen now affiliated with the IWW. Rather, it sought to guarantee the loyalty of the minority of "white" firemen and prevent them from leaving to join the rival union.

Opposition

The commitment to revolutionary syndicalism of the core group of Spanish immigrants did not extend to all workers or anarchists. Individualist anarchists remained skeptical about the usefulness of organizations such as unions in creating a truly libertarian society. Among Spanish immigrant anarchists, Dionisio Freijomil and Manuel Rey engaged in union organizing, either in the Unión de Fogoneros or the IWW, while others such as Juan Anido and Jesús Louzara strongly criticized these tactics.

The first important diatribe came in the individualist anarchist newspaper *El Único*, published in the Panama Canal Zone. Manuel D. Rodríguez, a Galician migrant and a leading proponent of this strain of anarchism, viciously attacked the union model of the Unión de Fogoneros, especially the Galician members, whom he called *chupópteros* (bloodsuckers). Freijomil was among those targeted, but he soon left the Unión de Fogoneros to promote the individualist group Lucifer. In contrast to the trade unionism and syndicalism promoted by the group that published *Cultura Obrera*, Rodríguez proposed an autonomous organization without stable coordination or representational structures, and he even promoted an alternative collective of maritime workers in Panama called the Centro Brisas Libertarias.[93]

He rejected the union structure and proposed that workers organize themselves on each ship, independently of the others, to avoid hierarchization. Rodríguez and the Federación Individualista de Panamá (Individualist Federation of Panama) did not represent the center of Spanish-language anarchist thought that flowed through a network with Havana as its hub. Rather, it illustrates the breadth of this radical world. José Galán responded to Rodríguez from Galicia on behalf of the Unión de Fogoneros. His response expressed the deep frustration of many union members, caught in the middle of a doctrinal debate that could hinder labor organizing to the benefit of the shipping companies.[94] Martínez de la Graña also responded by defending the organizing of workers, however conservative the organization might be, to carry out libertarian and syndicalist propaganda among them.[95]

Individualist criticism of the Unión de Fogoneros was not limited to the newspaper in Panama. It also appeared in the North American Atlantic ports, sometimes reproducing Rodríguez's vitriol with direct attacks on personal integrity. The primary target of these insinuations, distilled in port café conversations, was Martínez de la Graña. He alluded to some of these attacks in his own articles published in *Cultura Obrera* with irony and sarcasm: "After a few weeks of waiting for these ports, we have once again received our beloved *Cultura Obrera*, a weekly newspaper that our enemies, the shippers, wish to see dead and buried, and its publishers turned into minced meat enough to make chorizos, and, even more so, that devilish stutterer [Martínez de la Graña] who doesn't waste a week without blaming them for their misdeeds."[96]

Confrontation with individualists continued through 1912 and 1913. Sometimes it did so in a more ambiguous way, such as an article that Martínez de la Graña dedicated to Freijomil and his colleagues in the Lucifer collective. Perhaps out of respect for Freijomil's organizing in the early days of the Unión de Fogoneros, Martínez de la Graña only complained about Freijomil's poor work ethic and his supposed fondness for salon activism.[97] Other core Unión de Fogoneros organizers, such as Juan Naya, harshly criticized the divisive and obstructionist attitude of the individualists and the dire consequences they had for union activism within the Union itself: "All that you of the Lucifer group have done is in sight; your rebelliousness and discontent have only served to divide into two sides."[98]

The attacks against Martínez de la Graña were neither casual nor anecdotal. Attacking him struck at the heart of Unión de Fogoneros organizing because, despite him not serving in an official capacity, he was one of its more active supporters. He volunteered his services for administrative functions, coordination, and collaboration. He also wrote a regular column in its newspaper.[99] His rigid and occasionally dogmatic but incorruptible language and attitude made him a target for harassment, and a campaign to discredit him ultimately set its sights on the entire union.

Rupture with the ISU and incorporation into the IWW

In April 1913, the Unión de Fogoneros definitively broke with the ISU and affiliated with the Industrial Workers of the World through its Marine Transport Workers industrial union (MTW).

Surviving documents do not allow us to know the precise number of firemen and oilers who changed cards at this time by exchanging their blue notebook for the Wobblies' red card. Many leaders in the old organization strongly favored joining the IWW and believed its mission of organizing workers across race and language would be especially effective in the world of maritime labor. There is also evidence that the departure of firemen significantly weakened the ISU.[100]

Cultura Obrera became an official organ of the IWW and advanced its views about industrial organization. The content continued to include reports of supporters and causes deserving support. Jaime Vidal synthesized its principles in articles that discussed strategic positioning as the paper continued its pedagogical function, and its readership reached into the thousands.[101] While shipboard subscribers continued, the number from inland cities without ports increased, indicating the broadening reach of the paper but also suggesting continued difficulty organizing in ports as reports of job actions decreased.[102]

The split was felt by Unión de Fogoneros's members and leaders, as was clearly expressed in the pages of *Cultura Obrera*: "We are more dead than alive, we have completely disappeared from the organized workers' world."[103] This atmosphere of defeat weighed heavily on the spirits of Unión de Fogoneros leaders, but it did not prevent repeated calls for the reorganization of the firemen in 1914. There was no explicit appeal for the recovery of the old union. The widespread apathy may have been reflected in the large number of workers who returned to Spain in these years.

Martínez de la Graña saw the realignment with bitterness and resentment from his new home port of Boston. "We do not care about the American Federation of Labor or about the Industrial Workers of the World because, speaking clearly, for me they are the same as each other, since the same leaders feel the same ambitions and both take little or no care of those of us who are continually in daily battle."[104] Martínez de la Graña distanced his position from these two major North American unions to promote an alternative organizational model in which both the maritime trades and the naval districts (Atlantic, Great Lakes, Gulf, and Pacific) would be unified to use the general strike as a pressure mechanism. Although Martínez de la Graña remained affiliated with the MTW, in practice he distanced himself from the organization and criticized the "hierarchical" functioning of the IWW from the pages of the anarchist newspaper *Fuerza Consciente*. However, he continued to occasionally collaborate with the group around *Cultura Obrera*, and available evidence seems to indicate that he oriented his work toward social solidarity activities rather than union organizing, explicitly turning away from the orientation chosen by the Unión de Fogoneros.[105]

Jaime Vidal and Pedro Esteve were the two primary advocates of the Unión de Fogoneros affiliating with the IWW. In late 1913 or early 1914, Vidal relocated to California, first to Los Angeles and then to San Francisco, accompanied by José Vilariño, an affiliate of the Unión de Fogoneros who occasionally worked as the administrator of *Cultura Obrera*. They had begun publishing a new anarchist newspaper in New York called *Brazo y Cerebro* (*Arm and Brain*) in 1912. They renamed the paper *Fuerza Consciente* in 1913 and continued publishing it in California. They definitively moved away from maritime unionism with the new newspaper and their relocation. *Fuerza Consciente* became a new voice of militant Spanish-language anarchism in the United States. For example, in April 1914 Vidal and Vilariño, along with fifteen other Spanish anarchists, promoted a new anarchist group in San Francisco called the Propaganda Expropiadora, which advocated for "direct action and expropriating action of producers."[106]

Existing sources, notably articles in the newspaper *Fuerza Consciente*, do not explain the reason for their departure for the West Coast. The year prior, Vidal defended syndicalist organizing as a model for maritime workers and advocated its revolutionary potential. Vidal, however, also believed in the theoretical justification for violent forms of class resistance against the capitalist system. His militance may have led to his departure.

Whatever the reasons, Vidal continued his close association with *Cultura Obrera*, and the two newspapers frequently collaborated by advertising each other and occasionally shared articles by, for example, Emilio Gante or Juan Uriarte. Martínez de la Graña also gradually reduced his work on *Cultura Obrera*, and in his place new staff took on responsibilities. The Galician Francisco López García, who often went by "José Marinero" in the pages of *Cultura Obrera*, stood out among the new faces. López García, an anarchist based in Boston who occasionally worked at sea, brought personal connections to the mostly Italian anarchists in Luigi Galleani's group and its newspaper *Cronaca Sovversiva*. He chronicled international maritime workers in the regular *Cultura Obrera* column "De los Trabajadores del Mar" (Workers of the Sea) started by Martínez de la Graña. The bylines of historical leaders of the Union de Fogoneros, such as José Filgueira, Genaro Pazos, and Antonio Ucha, and new voices, including Manuel Alfaya and Juan Recio, frequently appeared next to López García's name.

Economic crisis and the consequent loss of jobs also pushed many Spanish seafarers to make their way back home or, for those who decided to stay in the United States, to look for work in factories or fields. In a note calling for an assembly of firemen in New York on July 13, 1914, the warning signs became evident. "It is essential to get out of the morass in which we find ourselves. Under these conditions it is not possible to continue. If you really hate the servitude and exploitation to which you are subjected, if you want to put yourself in a state of being able to fight it, if you love to be treated like men, you must worry more about your organization."[107] Two years later, however, the picture seemed to have changed radically. In August 1916, Spanish firemen Herminio Gutiérrez acknowledged his surprise at the progress made, both morally and materially, in the previous thirteen months and that the work of reorganization was progressing steadily, including the incorporation of "five to six thousand members in the union" and salary increases. He went on to explain that perhaps the best evidence of organizational recovery was that Spanish anarchists in the Atlantic ports in May 1917 promoted a call for firemen to strike that the rival ISU openly fought and hired scabs against. However, Gutiérrez recognized that they had not been able to reactivate those he defined as "the convinced." He referred to old anarchists, and certain individuals who had been delegates, presidents or secretaries, as "great fighters who are nowhere to be seen."[108]

We do not know if this broad criticism was also directed against Martínez de la Graña. The close link between Spanish anarchists and the Unión de Fogoneros weakened, and, although Martínez de la Graña always remained loyal to the libertarian cause, he considerably reduced his agitation. He disappeared from Unión de Fogoneros headquarters, and with this his sharp mind expressed through his writing was no longer in evidence, although those who knew him and had read his writings carried a sense of devotion toward him.

Global connections

Manuel Alfaya is particularly interesting because he suddenly appeared on the maritime unionism scene during the World War I period, linked to the Unión de Fogoneros while acting as a leader of the MTW in the ports of Norfolk and Boston. Born on July 15, 1890, Alfaya emigrated to Argentina in May 1906, departing from Vigo, Spain, and arriving in Buenos Aires on the *Cap Blanco*. A few months after arrival in Argentina he moved to Rosario where he worked as a maritime fireman and joined the libertarian movement. In 1916 he left Argentina and settled in Boston.

He was an active contributor to anarchist newspapers such as *Tierra y Libertad, La Protesta*, and *Cultura Obrera* between 1917 and 1918. In May 1918 he became secretary of the MTW in Boston. He maintained an active transnational profile that reveals the role played by Unión de Fogoneros organizers in the dissemination of the principles of revolutionary unionism in South America. In his capacity as maritime leader he maintained regular contacts with Argentine and Chilean trade union organizations, in addition to collaborating with the anarchist newspaper *La Protesta*.

Alfaya represented the MTW's base of Spanish, Mexican, Peruvian, and Argentine firemen. His work saw him embark on steamers traveling along Atlantic trade routes, which allowed him to serve as a union courier between the different ports of call. In May 1918, US postal authorities confiscated five copies of the Argentine anarchist newspaper *La Rebelión* sent to Alfaya while he was secretary of the MTW in Boston. In November 1919, a federal agent intercepted copies of a Chilean anarchist newspaper sent to a "Spanish anarchist unionist of the IWW" (Alfaya).[109] Authorities arrested him under the Sedition Act as a "dangerous anarchist," and he was eventually sentenced to deportation to Spain by a federal order issued on January 28, 1919, though, in the end, he was not deported.[110]

In 1919, Genaro Pazos, another Unión de Fogoneros leader, exchanged letters with the Spanish-born IWW member Gabriel Malvido in Buenos Aires. They discussed ways to coordinate worker mobilization in their locations and the incorporation of maritime workers into the IWW in Chile through propaganda carried out by Galician sailors in Valparaiso.[111] The large contingent of Spanish sailors formed an effective information network along the Atlantic and Pacific in this period.[112]

For his part, Martínez de la Graña joined the Galician fraternal organization Club Coruña in 1923. The club was founded in New York in 1903, integrated into the Hispanic American Center. Martínez de la Graña had been very critical of ethnic

126

associations in the past, but he apparently changed course. He also expanded his social relationships and befriend the much-despised café owner Gerardo Moscoso. *Fuerza Consciente* published an alert to workers, telling of Martínez de la Graña's move away from the workers' movement in 1914, but a similar warning did not appear in *Cultura Obrera*, then an official organ of the IWW.[113] Martínez de la Graña's death in 1928 came as he fell victim to an accident on a floating crane. His opponents did not celebrate his death. The conservative Spanish-language New York daily *La Prensa*, a relentless critic of the Unión de Fogoneros and Spanish anarchists, dedicated its cover to him and highlighted the extreme coherence with which he lived his life as a defender of the rights of maritime workers. Some of his still-devoted comrades living in Spain composed an obituary full of emotion and respect. There is some symbolism in his death as it marked a time when the union slid further into its decline before disappearing.[114]

The IWW faced severe repression in the United States after the country entered World War I in 1917. Though it managed continued spurts of workplace organizing after the war and through the 1920s, much of its organizing concentrated on prisoner support into the early 1920s. It also continued its international focus.

The 1910s were particularly important to the anarchist movement across the Americas. The historian Jennifer Guglielmo writes that the New York–metropolitan area provided a dynamic environment for the radical movement as one of the most important global centers of radical diaspora. Newly arrived immigrants jointly sponsored demonstrations, picnics, and other collective mobilizations to build solidarity and raise awareness about (and funds for) political prisoners, strikers, and their newspapers, among other causes.[115] Many of the Spanish-speaking migrants who arrived in New York and worked in the maritime sector or tobacco industry joined anarchist groups or unions with ethnic or language concentrations. They established new transnational connections between their places of origin, new places of residence, and locations along the way. *Cultura Proletaria* and *Cultura Obrera*, two radical publications edited by Spanish anarchists, played a fundamental role in the development of the Spanish-language network, with Pedro Esteve's guidance and influence.[116]

Anarcho-syndicalists in New York established a close alliance with the anarchist group that published *¡Tierra!* in Havana. They formed a common organizing center, separate from the anarcho-syndicalism advanced by *La Protesta* in Buenos Aires. *La Protesta*, *¡Tierra!*, and *Cultura Obrera* defended the need for organization, although in different forms. The close cooperation between New York and Havana manifested itself in economic support for their respective publications. They cooperated in their support campaigns for Alejandro Aldamas. In addition, they supported anarchists facing government repression in Cuba and the Mexican revolutionaries of the Partido Liberal Mexicano.

New York also offered temporary refuge for Mexican anarchists and trade unionists through their close personal and organizational relationship with the *Cultura Obrera* group. The Spanish immigrant anarchists who formed the Germinal group in 1915 had fled Mexico and the repression that followed Venustiano Carranza's ascendency to the presidency. The group published a newspaper under the same name, *Germinal*, again a reference to the Zola novel.[117] While relocating to New York improved their personal safety, it proved difficult for them to continue organizing. In November 1916, the PLM newspaper *Regeneración* reported that the Germinal group had ceased publishing its newspaper and dissolved as an organization, at least in part due to repression by the US government. Some of the core group returned to Tampico, Mexico, and launched the new weekly newspaper *Tribuna Roja*.[118]

As often was the case, the distance between desire and reality revealed itself through actual organizing. In November 1911, the Spanish anarchist Antonio Loredo, exiled in Montevideo, requested support from the Unión de Fogoneros in New York, asking them to refuse to handle goods from or for Argentina, on behalf of the Comité Pro-Libertades Argentinas.[119] Loredo viewed this kind of transnational labor solidarity as crucial to the fight against the enforcement of the Ley de Residencia in Argentina. The Unión de Fogoneros response showed the enormous gulf between desires of a universal movement and the limitations of their organization. An uncredited article in *Cultura Obrera*, presumably written by Pedro Esteve, viewed this proposal as nothing more than "a beautiful aspiration." Rather than striking and facing the repercussions, workers would be best served by continuing to build a world transport federation and integrating maritime and port workers, taking as a model the Federation of Port Workers that had been established in New York in 1909.[120] This line of argument showed strains of realism among the publishers of *Cultura Obrera*.

Conclusion

As Geoffroy de Laforcade reminds us, formal or revolutionary political ideologies and their principles cannot be abstracted from the experiences lived by those who interpreted and appropriated them. Nor can they be separated from the understanding of the symbolic social contexts and spatial locations that they framed.[121] People living and working in these spaces relied on their locally situated knowledge to mobilize and resist.[122] It is crucial to locate these spaces of resistance because they allow us to interpret the meaning of worker organizations in the context of their oppression and marginalization.

In the case of Spanish migrant maritime workers in the United States, these were the ports, docks, and ships, in addition to the relational spaces—the contact zones as conceptualized by Winston James—where they experienced racism and developed a sense of belonging to a differentiated group. Group formation occurred on a connected yet distinct pathway to their understanding themselves as workers in a stratified economic system; they developed tools to collectively organize to improve their lives along both lines.[123]

It is a testament to their strength of will and skills as organizers that so many workers with precarious work and living conditions formed a union of such strength. The small group of Spanish anarchists and firemen at the core of this group drove its formation and propelled its global connections. The Unión de Fogoneros's incorporation into the ISU stands as a significant moment in US labor history for the inclusion of such a radical syndicalist union within a craft union body. The firemen surely viewed the ISU as a lever to maximize their strength. Perhaps the ISU did not view the firemen's revolutionary outlook as threatening and cooperated with the Spanish firemen for their own benefit, but clearly this period illustrates the ideological and racial lines of the US labor movement blurring. Although the Unión de Fogoneros did not survive long—it virtually disappeared in 1926—it offers a unique perspective with which to analyze transnationalism's maritime connections. The union was unique in its desire to build a single organization in the maritime world and to use the general strike as a revolutionary instrument against the capitalist system.

Epilogue

Most Spanish maritime workers evade our efforts to reconstruct their lives for reasons connected to their marginalization. Michel-Rolph Trouillot argued that power imbalances silence the past by impeding source creation and later decisions about which sources to preserve in archives.[1] For instance, there is evidence suggesting the importance of Galician migrants in Uruguay's maritime sector. Galicians were the largest group of workers in the industry, but we lack documents detailing their participation. Better sources allow a fuller picture of the organizing trajectory at the Port of Buenos Aires and, now through this book, the contributions of the anarchist Constante Carballo. In Argentina, Cuba, and New York, Spanish immigrant anarchists shaped their world through their print culture, which provides historians today with a vital lens into their organizing and lives.

Uncovering this past world of radical organizing gives us a base to write both a comparative and joint history of Spanish immigrant maritime workers in the American Atlantic. The history explored in each chapter's geographic focus area is interconnected through migrant flows, trade, and globalization, while also being locally rooted, requiring reflection on the political and social worlds in each area.[2] In this sense, our work aspired to compare these locations while also rising to become a history of Spanish immigrant maritime workers in the Atlantic.

Anton Rosenthal documents the IWW's geographical reach through the mobility of people and ideas through newspapers, which contributed to the global dissemination of revolutionary theory and practice.[3] This characterization also applies to the activities of Spanish maritime organizing along Atlantic coasts of North and South America. Movement typified most agitators' lives. Their organizing grew from their decisions to migrate and from the continued mobility of their working lives, sailing from port to port on the vessels on which they labored.

Physical movement across geographies broadened their intellectual horizons by exposing them to new ideas and perspectives and facilitating the exchange of ideas between workers. In this sense, maritime work is a perfect paradigm of the transnational ideal. In Argentina, for example, workers organized unrestrained by national demarcations when they established connections with Brazilian, Uruguayan, and Paraguayan workers to create a shared space of labor struggle.

The reforms sought by Juan Arévalo, the leading advocate for Cuban maritime workers to join the Pan-American organization, illustrate a different window into transnationalism, this time one of an unequal relationship between Cuban workers and the AFL in the United States. This contrasts with the anarchists in Cuba who forged solidarities with anarchists in Central America and the East Coast of the United States. The Spanish anarchist José María Blázquez de Pedro sought to build a libertarian continental network, however unsuccessful it may have been.

Transnationalism was constantly present in the organizing activities of Spanish maritime workers in the United States. In New York, the anarchists who led the Unión de Fogoneros shaped a radical network throughout the Atlantic Coast that reached into the Gulf of Mexico and the southern United States. The union always stressed the need for a truly global organization to unify all the radical maritime unions around the world that would coordinate action for a universal general strike.

Global perspectives intertwined with local organizing. In the ports of Buenos Aires, Havana, and New York, union organizers created spaces of resistance to capitalism and promoted their visions for social progress. Their cultural work in social centers, assemblies, and meetings in their headquarters, and the relentless criticism of their compatriots who exploited their scant organizing resources in narrow "ethnic" organizing, all reflect this global view. The newspapers they published served as spaces of resistance against government repression and were largely free from the omnipresent workplace control exercised by abusive employers.[4]

Precarity also typified the lives of maritime workers. Many worked seasonally and filled the temporary needs of employers, frequently changing jobs and relying on their mobility to survive and scrape out a living in Buenos Aires, Havana, and the North American Atlantic Coast. Recovering this history makes evident transregional similarities. Resistance societies predominated in early organizing, which then rolled into larger syndicalist unions. Maritime unions expanded in the first decade of the twentieth century. In Argentina these efforts consolidated in the Federación Obrera Marítima, first organized in 1910, and in the United States in the IWW's Marine Transport Workers in 1913. Cuba followed a similar process from nascent organizing to institutionalization, although with different ideological positions.

Though the maritime labor movements across the Americas shared broad similarities through their participation in global leftist currents, each location followed distinct paths based on their local political, economic, and cultural positions. Decisions about if and how to negotiate with employers, or to accept state mediation in a strike, by necessity reflected temporal and jurisdictionally bounded factors. Spanish maritime workers in

Argentina, Cuba, and New York faced different forms of capitalism and different governing regimes in different states with distinct populations. Workers with similar backgrounds to migrants from Spain across the Atlantic articulated their movements through their experiences.

Mobile agitators moved through these differences as they transited between locations of struggle. Argentine and broader Latin American anarcho-syndicalist history is full of people spreading radical ideals along the path of their travels, similar to their predecessors like Errico Malatesta and Pietro Gori. Constante Carballo, Juan Martínez de la Graña, and Jaime Vidal, among others, personified the continuity of this agitator model from different ideological coordinates. Carballo, for example, connected the Río de la Plata and the south of Brazil through the organizational solidarity of maritime workers; he helped create a transnational movement.

Kirwin Shaffer writes about Spanish-language anarchist networks across Tampa, Puerto Rico, Cuba, and through the Caribbean. This was part of a wider network that stretched into Mexico and the US ports of New York, Norfolk, Philadelphia, Boston, and New Orleans, in addition to the Southwestern US.[5] Kenyon Zimmer characterizes anarchism in the late-nineteenth century and early-twentieth centuries as "a movement *in* movement." "It was also a movement *of* movements," he adds, "worldwide in scale but composed of overlapping groups and networks loosely demarcated by characteristics such as location, language, and nationality."[6] In similar terms, the anarchist and syndicalist movements spread and supported each other through their networks, but these movements were also made up of networks of networks that variously were overlaid and interlocked with each other. Martha Ackelsberg highlights the importance that railways, international mail services, and other communication forms had for anarchists, as models of networks that provided services to people without the authorities' intervention to configure these networks.[7] Engineers have a similar conceptualization of "systems of systems," which describe "large-scale distributed systems" made up of "components" that are "complex systems themselves."[8]

Maritime labor organizers of all stripes used the network function of merchant marine flows in Argentina, Cuba, and the United States to grow their movements. This was similar to what Ackelsberg describes as a "federative network" to define the coordinated action of local anarchist groups.[9] This configuration, in which neither local groups nor more broadly coordinated structures could speak or act on behalf of others, was especially valued by the Spanish anarcho-syndicalists based on the North American Atlantic Coast. Strongly influenced by Kropotkin's thought, Pedro Esteve's views on "voluntary associations" defended the autonomy of local sections and rejected "management organizations" or leaders detached from productive work.

In addition, most anarchists, militants, and trade unionists had little organizing experience prior to migrating. They learned and developed organizing strategies during the mobilizations and conflicts in each of the local maritime sectors. Defending workers' control was a central element of maritime unionist militancy.[10] This came about because of the strategic position of workers in this key economic sector. Labor organizers placed great emphasis on the power of workers as producers, and on ships and ports as spaces to realize new relationships and freedoms. Anarcho-syndicalist agitators emphasized the importance of union control over the workplace, whether on docks or onboard ships. These ideals gave theoretical and political support to extending workers' control of the means of production that would then serve as a base for a new and hopefully better society.[11]

Notes

Introduction

1. Peter Linebaugh and Marcus Rediker, *The Many-Headed Hydra: Sailors, Slaves, Commoners, and the Hidden History of the Revolutionary Atlantic* (Boston: Beacon Press, 2000), 19.
2. Michel-Rolph Trouillot, *Silencing the Past: Power and the Production of History* (Boston: Beacon Press, 1995), 23.
3. Much of the focus of labor and working-class history over prior decades, specifically the attention to the history of anarchism, focused on recovering these stories.
4. Trouillot, *Silencing the Past.*
5. Antonio Antelo Iglesias, "El Atlántico en la historia y la leyenda," in *Espacio Tiempo y Forma*, Serie III, Historia Medieval, 1993; K. Rodríguez Wittmann, "La visión cartográfica del Atlántico en el siglo XVI: Notas entorno al ejemplar del Theatrum Orbis Terrarum conservado en el Fondo Antiguo de la Universidad de La Laguna," XXII Coloquio de Historia Canario-Americana, 2018, xxii-089; Ángel Luis Cervera Fantoni, *Historia Naval de España* (Córdoba: Sekotia, 2023); David González Cruz, *Barcos y construcción naval entre el Atlántico y el Mediterráneo en la época de los descubrimientos (siglos XV y XVI)* (Madrid: Consejo Superior de Investigaciones Científicas, 2018); Eduard Le Daunois, *El Atlántico: historia y vida de un océano* (Madrid: Espasa Calpe,

1943); Mario Hernández Sánchez-Barba, *El mar en la historia de América* (Madrid: Editorial MAPFRE, 1992).

6. César Yáñez Gallardo, *La emigración española a América, siglos XIX y XX, dimensión y características cuantitativas* (Colombres: Archivo de Indianos, 1994); Germán Rueda Hernanz y Consuelo Soldevilla Oria, *Españoles emigrantes en América, siglos XVI–XX* (Madrid: Arco Libros, 2000); Consuelo Naranjo Orovio, *Las migraciones de España a Ibero américa desde la Independencia* (Madrid: Libros de la Catarata, 2020); Germán Rueda Hernanz, *La emigracion contemporanea de espanoles a Estados Unidos, 1820–1950: De "dons" a "Misteres"* (Madrid: Editorial MAPFRE, 1993); Nicolás Sánchez-Albornoz, *Españoles hacia América: La emigraciónen masa, 1880–1930* (Madrid: Alianza Editorial, 1988).

7. Bernard Bailyn, *Atlantic History. Concept and Contours* (Boston: Harvard University Press, 2009); Jack P. Greene and Philip D. Morgan, eds., *Atlantic History. A Critical Appraisal* (Oxford: Oxford University Press, 2008); Wim Klooster, *Revolutions in the Atlantic World: A Comparative History* (New York: New York University Press, 2009); Willem Klooster and Alfred Padula, *The Atlantic World: Essays on Slavery, Migration and Imagination* (New York: Routledge, 2018); Marcus Rediker, *The Slave Ship* (New York: Penguin, 2007); Marcus Rediker, *Villains of All Nations: Atlantic Pirates in the Golden Age* (London: Verso, 2020).

8. David Armitage, "Tres Conceptos de Historia Atlántica," *Revista de Occidente* 281 (2004): 15.

9. See, for instance, Marco Mariano, ed., *Defining the Atlantic Community: Culture, Intellectuals, and Policies in the Mid-Twentieth Century* (New York: Routledge, 2010), 6–7.

10. Armitage, "Tres Conceptos," 24.

11. Armitage, "Tres Conceptos," 26.

12. Isabel Hofmeyr, "AHR Conversations: on Transnational History," *American Historical Review* (December 2006): 1454.

13. Geoffroy de Laforcade and Kirwin Shaffer, eds., *In Defiance of Boundaries: Anarchism in Latin American History* (Gainesville: University Press of Florida, 2015); Peter Cole, David Struthers, and Kenyon Zimmer, eds., *Wobblies of the World: A Global History of the IWW* (London: Pluto Press, 2017).

14. Translated from Lourenzo Fernández Prieto, "Historia transfronteriza, historia transnacional, el espacio de la historia," paper presented at Encuentros por la Historia, Universidad Nacional, Heredia, Costa Rica, August 1999, 10.

15. Steven Hirsch and Lucien Van der Walt, eds., *Anarchism and Syndicalism in the Colonial and Postcolonial World, 1870–1940: The Praxis of National Liberation, Internationalism, and Social Revolution* (Boston: Brill, 2010).

16. Jack London, *Revolution, and Other Essays* (New York: Macmillan, 1910), 146.

17. Francisco Comín, *Historia Económica Mundial: De losorígenes a la actualidad* (Madrid: Alianza Editorial, 2012), 452.

18. Kevin H. O'Rourke and Jeffrey G. Williamson, "When Did Globalisation Begin?," *European Review of Economic History* 6, no. 1 (April 2002): 37.

19. O'Rourke and Williamson, "When Did Globalisation Begin?," 38.

20. Enric García, "La mecanización en la marina mercante española: Los marineros ante el cambio tecnológico, 1870–1914," *Revista de Historia Industrial* 65 (2016): 71.

21. García, "La mecanización en la marina mercante española," 59.

22. Eric W. Sager, *Seafaring Labour: The Merchant Marine of Atlantic Canada, 1820–1914* (Montreal: McGill-Queen's University Press, 1989), 263.

23. García, "La mecanización en la marina mercante española," 64.

24. Jesús María Valdaliso, "Las navieras española seneles pejo británico (c. 1860– c. 1914): La transferencia de capitales, sistemas de gestión y modelos de financiaciónenunaindustriainternacionalizada," *Transportes, Servicios y Telecomunicaciones*, no 13 (December 2007), 106.

25. J. Zamora Terrés, *Notas para una historia del movimiento obrero en la Marina mercante* (Barcelona: Museu Marítim de Barcelona, 2003), 2.

26. Zamora Terrés, *Notas para una historia del movimiento obrero*, 3.

27. Marcus Rediker, *Between the Devil and the Deep Blue Sea: Merchant Seamen, Pirates and the Anglo-American Maritime World, 1700–1750* (Cambridge: Cambridge University Press, 1989), 339–40.

28. Garcia, "La mecanización en la marina mercante española," 55.

29. Bruce Nelson, *Workers on the Waterfront: Seamen, Longshoremen, and Unionism in the 1930s* (Urbana: University of Illinois Press, 1990), 16.

30. "How sad, on the other hand, to be at the bottom of that ship, under the water, with no more horizon or task than to feed the

voracious furnaces that set in motion that monster that crosses the seas! There's nothing appetizing there. It's all hard, the work, the deal, the bed. Not even what happens in the ship is known." Editorial, "Lo que somos y a lo que aspiramos" *Cultura Obrera* (Brooklyn), November 4, 1911.

31. Nelson, *Workers on the Waterfront*, 18.
32. Translated from Eduardo Zamacois, *La alegria de andar: Croquis de un viaje por tierras de Puerto Rico y Cuba, Estados Unidos, Centro-América y América del Sur (1916–1920)* (Madrid: Renacimiento, 1920), 40.
33. Javier Moreno Rico, "Condiciones de vida y de trabajo en la Marina Mercante de cimonónica," *Revista de historia naval* 115 (2011): 13.
34. Moreno Rico, "Condiciones de vida y de trabajoen," 284.
35. Xan da Graña, "Para los fogoneros de Boston," *Cultura Obrera*, June 28, 1913.
36. Rediker, *Between the Devil and the Deep Blue Sea*, 294.
37. Nelson, *Workers on the Waterfront*, 14; "El salvajismo en Estados Unidos: Tripulación a tropellada en el vapor *Apache*," *Cultura Proletaria*, July 30, 1910.
38. Translated from *La Unión del Marino* (Buenos Aires), January 1921.
39. José Fernández, "Desde el 'Brutus,'" *Cultura Obrera*, November 4, 1911.
40. Winston James, "Culture, Labor, and Race in The Shadow of U.S. Capital," in Stephan Palmié and Francisco A. Scarano, eds., *The Caribbean: A History of the Region and Its Peoples* (Chicago: University of Chicago Press, 2011), 450.
41. Kevin A. Yelvington, "Caribbean Crucible: History, Culture, and Globalization," https://prallagon.com/wp-content/uploads/2021/01/Caribbean-People-History-Culture.pdf; Winston James, *Holding Aloft the Banner of Ethiopia: Caribbean Radicalism in Early-Twentieth Century America* (Brooklyn: Verso Books, 2020), 71.
42. James, *Holding Aloft the Banner of Ethiopia*, 82.
43. Translated from Juan Martínez, "Crónica de Fogoneros," *Cultura Obrera*, October 6, 1911.
44. Peter Cole, *Dockworker Power: Race and Activism in Durban and the San Francisco Bay Area* (Urbana: University of Illinois Press, 2018), 5.
45. Alice Mah, *Port Cities and Global Legacies: Urban Identity,*

Waterfront Work, and Radicalism (London: Palgrave Macmillan, 2014), 179.

Chapter 1: Life on the Docks

1. Marcel Van der Linden and Wayne Thorpe, *Revolutionary Syndicalism: An International Perspective* (London: Scholar Press, 1990), 29.
2. Noemí M. Girbal-Blacha, "Perfiles históricos de la Argentina rural: Agro y política (1880–1970)," *Historia: Debates y tendencias* 16, no. 1 (2016): 17–36.
3. Michael Miller, *Europe and the Maritime World: A Twentieth Century History* (Cambridge: Cambridge University Press, 2012), 81.
4. Girbal-Blacha, "Perfiles históricos de la Argentina rural," 17–36.
5. Mario Rapoport, "Etapas y crisis en la historia económica Argentina (1880–2005)," *Oikos: Revista de la Escuela de Administración y Economía*, no. 21 (2006).
6. Rapoport, "Etapas y crisis."
7. Laura Caruso, "La huelga, el carnaval y los comicios: El mundo del trabajo portuario en Buenos Aires y la configuración de una comunidad obrera, verano de 1904," *Historia Crítica*, no. 73 (2019): 163–91; Laura Caruso, "Huelga a bordo: Los orígenes de la FOM en 1910 y el sindicalismo revolucionario," *Revista de Estudios Marítimos y Sociales*, no. 5/6 (2012/2013): 91–102; Laura Caruso, "'Onde manda capitão, não governa marinheiro'? O trabalho marítimo no rio da Prata, 1890–1920," *Revista Mundos do Trabalho* 2, no. 3 (August 2010); Lucas Poy and Laura Caruso, "Las huelgas del Riachuelo: Los primeros conflictos obreros en el puerto de Buenos Aires, 1889 y 1895," *Revista Mundos do Trabalho* 4, no. 7 (November 2012); Laura Caruso, *Embarcados: Los trabajadores marítimos y la vida a bordo: Sindicato, empresas y Estado en el puerto de Buenos Aires, 1889–1921* (Buenos Aires: Imago Mundi, 2016).
8. Ricardo Falcón, *El mundo del trabajourbano: 1890–1914* (Buenos Aires: Centro Editor de América Latina, 1986), 62; Caruso, *Embarcados*, 73.
9. Poy and Caruso, "Las huelgas del Riachuelo."
10. Caruso, *Embarcados*, 31–32.
11. Caruso, "La huelga, el carnaval y los comicios," 16.

12. Laura Caruso, "Tripulantes del sur: Trabajo y condiciones laborales en la navegación mercante argentina (1890–1920)," *Drassana*, no. 24 (2016): 29.

13. Ofelia Pianetto, "Mercado de trabajo y acción sindical en la Argentina, 1890–1922," *Desarrollo Económico* 24, no. 94, (July–September 1984): 297–307.

14. Eric Hobsbawm, *Trabajadores: Estudios de historia de la clase obrera* (Barcelona: Crítica, 1979), 222.

15. Caruso, "La huelga, el carnaval y los comicios," 16.

16. Aurelio González Climent and Anselmo González Climent, *Buenos Aires: Historia de la Marina Mercante Argentina*, vol. 4 ([Buenos Aires:] Negri, 1972).

17. Vitor Wagner Neto de Oliveira, "Movimiento obrero transnacional en el Cono Sur Americano a principios del siglo XX: Los marítimos de los ríos Paraná y Paraguay," *Revista de Estudios Marítimos y Sociales*, no. 14 (January 2019): 197.

18. Translated from Edgardo Bilsky, *La F.O.R.A. y el movimiento obrero*, vol. 1 (Buenos Aires: CEAL, 1985), 53.

19. Caruso, "La huelga, el carnaval y los comicios"; Geoffroy de Laforcade, "Community Traditions, Labor Insurgencies, and Argentine Shipyard Workers," in *In Defiance of Boundaries: Anarchism in Latin American History*, Geoffroy de Laforcade and Kirwin Shaffer, eds. (Gainesville: University Press of Florida, 2015).

20. Geoffroy de Laforcade, "Federative Futures: Waterways, Resistance Societies, and the Subversion of Nationalism in the Early 20th-Century Anarchism of the Río de la Plata Region," *EIAL* 22, no. 2, (2011): 83.

21. James, *Holding Aloft the Banner of Ethiopia*, 451.

22. Neto de Oliveira, "Movimiento obrero transnacional," 43.

23. Geoffroy de Laforcade, "Straddling the Nation and the Working World: Anarchism and Syndicalism on the Docks and Rivers of Argentina," in *Anarchism and Syndicalism in the Colonial and Postcolonial World, 1870–1940: The Praxis of National Liberation, Internationalism, and Social Revolution*, eds. Steven Hirsch and Lucien Van der Walt (Leiden: Brill, 2010), 330.

24. Gonzalo Zaragoza, *Anarquismo Argentino (1876–1902)* (Madrid: Ediciones de la Torre, 1996), 80.

25. J. Ángel Maquieira, *El anarquismo de Julio Camba* (Madrid: UNED, 2015), 80.

26. Zaragoza, *Anarquismo Argentino*, 95.

27. In Cristobal Maro's view, the action of this socialist workers group was fundamental to the organization of a significant number of resistance societies between 1894 and 1896. Cristóbal D. Maro, "Las estrategias socialistas para el movimiento obrero hacia fines del siglo XIX: Un estudio a partir de la biografía de Adrián Patroni," paper presented at VII Jornadas de Sociología, Facultad de Ciencias Sociales, Universidad de Buenos Aires, 2007, 13.

28. Ricardo Falcón states that "the Spanish group" was animated by Francisco Morales, Feliciano Rey, Gabriel Abad, and Zacarias Ravassa. Ricardo Falcón, *Los orígenes del movimiento obrero* (Buenos Aires: Centro Editor de América Latina, 1984), 122.

29. Horacio Tarcus, *Diccionariobiográfico de la izquierdaargentina* (Buenos Aires: Emecé Editores, 2007).

30. Lucas Poy and Sabrina Asquini, "La experiencia 'colectivista': Orígenes, desarrollo y alcances de la primera ruptura obrera en el Partido Socialista argentino, 1896–1900," in *PIMSA: Documentos y comunicaciones* (Buenos Aires), 2015.

31. Poy and Caruso, "Las huelgas del Riachuelo," 13.

32. Alejandro Belkin, *Sindicalismo revolucionario y movimiento obrero en la Argentina: De la gestación en el Partido Socialista a la conquista de la FORA (1900–1915)* (Buenos Aires: Imago Mundi—Ediciones CEHTI, 2018), 92.

33. Geoffroy de Laforcade, "Federative Futures: Waterways, Resistance Societies, and the Subversion of Nationalism in the Early 20th-Century Anarchism of the Río de la Plata Region," *EIAL* 22, no 2 (2011): 83.

34. Laforcade, "Federative Futures," 83.

35. Laforcade, "Federative Futures," 85.

36. Translated from Diego Abad de Santillán, *El movimiento anarquista en la Argentina* (Buenos Aires: Argonauta, 1930), 50.

37. Alejandro Belkin, *Sobre los orígenes del sindicalismo revolucionario en Argentina* (Buenos Aires: Centro Cultural de la Cooperación, Buenos Aires, 2007), 28.

38. Belkin, *Sobre los orígenes del sindicalismo revolucionario*, 205.

39. Iaácov Oved, *El Anarquismo y el movimiento obreroen la Argentina* (Buenos Aires: Siglo XXI, 1978), 236.

40. Oved, *El Anarquismo y el movimiento obreroen*, 252.

41. *La Protesta Humana*, October 13, 1902.

42. "En los puertos" *La Protesta Humana*, November 8, 1902.

43. Oved, *El Anarquismo y el movimiento obreroen*, 248–49.

44. Alejandro Andreassi Cieri, *La rebelión de los metecos: Conflictividad laboral y social en Buenos Aires, 1895–1910* (Barcelona: CIMS, 1997), 177–78.
45. "Desde Campana," *La Protesta Humana*, November 15, 1902.
46. Oved, *El Anarquismo y el movimiento obreroen*, 283.
47. Sebastián Marotta, *El movimiento sindical argentino: Su génesis y desarrollo*, vol. 2, *1907–1920* (Buenos Aires: Editorial Lacio, 1961), 103.
48. Laura Caruso, "Las hazañas del trabajo: protesta y solidaridadesen la huelga grande del Riachuelo, verano de 1904," in Mirta Lobato, ed., *Comunidades, historias locales y mundos del trabajo* (Buenos Aires: EDHASA, 2019), 170.
49. Caruso, "La huelga, el carnaval y los comicios," 37.
50. *La Vanguardia*, January 30, 1904; *La Prensa*, January 26, 1904.
51. *La Prensa*, January 9, 1904.
52. Caruso, "La huelga, el carnaval y los comicios," 41.
53. Martin Albornoz and Diego A. Galeano, "Los agitadores móviles: Trayectorias anarquistas y vigilancias portuarias en el Atlántico sudamericano, 1894–1908," *Almanack* (São Paulo: Universidade Federal de São Paulo, 2019): 21, 333.
54. Caruso, "La huelga, el carnaval y los comicios," 42.
55. Juan Suriano, "El estado argentino frente a los trabajadores urbanos: Política social y represión, 1880–1916," *Anuario*, no. 14 (1989–1990): 109–36.
56. Translated from Albornoz and Galeano, "Los agitadores móviles," 333–35.
57. Albornoz and Galeano, "Los agitadores móviles," 334.
58. Translated from "Informe de Víctor Valle al jefe de la División de Investigación Rossi, 11/01/1904." Cited in Caruso, "La huelga el carnaval y los comicios," 176.
59. Caruso, "La huelga el carnaval y los comicios," 176.
60. Marcela Aspell, "La Ley 4144 de Residencia: Antecedentes-Sanción-Aplicación," *Revista del Instituto del Derecho Ricardo Levene*, no. 25 (1979): 11–126; Iaácov Oved, "El trasfondo histórico de la ley 4.144, de Residencia," *Desarrollo Económico*, no 61, (1978), 123–51.
61. Albornoz and Galeano, "Los agitadores móviles," 334.
62. Albornoz and Galeano, "Los agitadores móviles," 335.
63. Albornoz and Galeano, "Los agitadores móviles," 337.
64. "Obreros estibadores y de ribera," *La Protesta*, August 10, 1904.

65. "Palestra: Más sobre el Congreso de Estibadores," *La Protesta*, September 10, 1904.
66. Caruso, *Embarcados*, 82.
67. Translated from "Estibadores y afines: La gira por los puertos," *La Protesta*, September 29, 1904.
68. "Marineros y foguistas: Un delegado brasileño," *La Protesta*, October 16, 1904; "Sociedade União dos Foguistas," *Jornal do Brasil*, February 25, 1904.
69. "Os estivadores," *Gazeta de Notícias*, October 23, 1904.
70. "Os estivadores," *Gazeta de Notícias*, October 23, 1904.
71. "Os estivadores," *Gazeta de Notícias*, October 23, 1904; "Reunião operária," *Jornal do Brasil*, October 24, 1904.
72. Translated from "Estibadores," *La Protesta*, October 25, 1904.
73. Translated from "Los obreros de los puertos," *La Protesta*, November 12, 1904.
74. Diego Abad de Santillán, *La FORA: Ideología y trayectoria del movimiento obrero revolucionario en la Argentina* (Buenos Aires: Libros de Anarres, 2005), 204.
75. *La Protesta*, November 22, 1904.
76. Translated from *La Protesta*, November 22, 1904.
77. "Triunfo en el Frigorífico La Blanca," *La Protesta*, November 24, 1904.
78. "Triunfo en el Frigorífico La Blanca," *La Protesta*, November 24, 1904.
79. "Las huelgas y la policía," *Revista de Policía*, no. 181 (December 1, 1904): 198.
80. "La huelga general," *La Protesta*, December 2, 1904.
81. Albornoz and Galeano, "Los agitadores móviles," 341.
82. Translated from Inés Rojkind, "La protestaen la calle: Visibilidad de la cuestión social en la ciudad del novecientos," paper presented at *Segundas Jornadas Nacionales de Historia Social*, May 13–15, 2009, La Falda, Córdoba, http://www.memoria.fahce .unlp.edu.ar/trab_eventos/ev.9709/ev.9709.pdf.
83. "Injurias graves," *La Organización Obrera*, December 1904.
84. "El terror en la República Argentina," *El Obrero*, February 21, 1905.
85. Francisco Corney, *Cuaderno de Notas*, manuscript cited in Albornoz and Galeano, "Los agitadores móviles," 343.
86. Translated from Alberto Ghiraldo, *La tiranía del frac* (Buenos Aires: Editorial La Protesta, 1905), 45.
87. Albornoz and Galeano, "Los agitadores móviles," 335.

88. Translated from Albornoz and Galeano, "Los agitadores móviles," 344.

89. "Telegramas. Argentina," *O Século*, July 18, 1905; Albornoz and Galeano, "Los agitadores móviles," 346.

90. Carlos Zubillaga, *Perfiles en sombra: Aportes a un diccionario biográfico de los orígenes del movimiento sindical en Uruguay (1870–1910)* (Montevideo: Librería de la Facultad de Humanidades y Ciencias de la Educación, 2008), 58.

91. Albornoz and Galeano, "Los agitadores móviles," 347.

92. "Deportados Argentinos," *La Protesta*, September 20, 1906; "Vergogne es infamie della Repubblica Argentina," *La Giustizia* (Montevideo), September 28, 1906.

93. "Y van. . . ," *La Protesta*, July 18, 1907.

94. Translated from "Y van. . . ," *La Protesta*, July 18, 1907.

95. Albornoz and Galeano, "Los agitadores móviles," 349.

96. "Al Pueblo," *Tribuna Libertaria* (Montevideo), July 28, 1907; "De Montevideo," *La Protesta,* July 31, 1907.

97. Translated from Albornoz and Galeano, "Los agitadores móviles," 350.

98. Letter of Ramón Falcón to the minister of the interior, August 2, 1907, in Albornoz and Galeano, "Los agitadores móviles," 350.

99. "Constante Carballo," *La Protesta*, August 8, 1907.

100. Translated from José Aricó, *La hipótesis de justo* (Buenos Aires: Sudamericana, 1998), 38.

101. Translated from Albornoz and Galeano, "Los agitadores móviles," 354.

102. In addition to his stay in the Southern Cone, Taboada closely followed the organizational model and activity of Spanish-speaking anarchists on the Atlantic coast of the United States. His writing appeared in a column titled "World Information" in several issues of New York's *Cultura Proletaria* throughout 1911 under the name Benito D'Raquea.

103. Óscar Freán Hernández, "Ideas y vidas a través del Atlántico: El anarquismo americano en la prensa libertaria gallega," *Historia y Política* 42 (2019): 124.

104. Eliseo Fernández and Dionisio Pereira, *O anarquismona Galiza* (Santiago de Compostela, Spain: Edicións Positivas, 2004), 254.

105. Fernández and Pereira, *O anarquismona Galiza.*

106. At 6:35 a.m. the day before the inauguration of the project, the steamers *Schliesen* and *Colombia* collided in the fog at the new

port, killing between sixty and one hundred passengers, causing the official opening celebration to be cancelled.

107. Pilar Cagiao Vila, "La inmigración gallega en Uruguay (1870–1936)," *Anuario americanista europeo*, no. 3 (2005): 93–112; "Montevideo, ciudad de inmigrantes: la presencia gallega (1870–1917)," in *Entre nós: estudios de arte, xeografía e historia en homenaxe ó profesor Xosé Manuel Pose Antelo*, ed. Xesús Balboa López and Herminia Pernas Oroza (Santiago de Compostela, Spain: Universidade de Santiago de Compostela, 2001), 491–506; Carlos Zubillaga, "La emigración gallega y los orígenes del sindicalismo uruguayo," *Galicia y América, el papel de la emigración: V Xornadas de Historia de Galicia*, ed. Jesús de Juana López and Xavier Castro Pérez (Orense, Spain: Servicio de Publicacións da Deputación Provincial de Ourense, 1990), 191–211.

108. Adela Pellegrino, *La población de Uruguay: Breve caracterización demográfica* (Montevideo: Fondo de Población de Naciones Unidas), 2010.

109. Gustavo Fernández, "Orígenes del movimiento sindical uruguayo," *Hemisferio Izquierdo*, no. 18 (September 2017), https://www.hemisferioizquierdo.uy/single-post/2017/09/18/or%C3%ADgenes-del-movimiento-sindical-uruguayo.

110. Abad de Santillán, *La FORA*, 135.

111. "De Montevideo: La gran huelga," *La Protesta*, May 30, 1905.

112. Laura Caruso, "Huelga a bordo: los orígenes de la FOM en 1910 y el sindicalism orevolucionario," *Revista de Estudios Marítimos y Sociales*, no. 5/6, (November 2012/2013): 95–97.

113. Laura Caruso, "La huelga general marítima del Puerto de Buenos Aires," *Revista de Estudios Marítimos y Sociales*, no. 1 (November 2008): 1–17.

114. Laura Caruso and Gustavo Contreras, "Jerárquicos y sindicalistas: Los orígenes del Centro de Capitanes de Ultramar y Oficiales de la Marina Mercanteen la Argentina (CCUOMM) de losaños de la primeraposguerra," *Transportes, Servicios y Telecomunicaciones*, no. 51 (2023): 75–110.

115. Belkin, *Sobre los orígenes del sindicalismo revolucionario*, 15.

116. Laura Caruso, and Gustavo Contreras, "Constelaciones gremiales en el mundo marítimo argentino: La Federación Obrera Marítima y el Centro de Capitanes de Ultramar (1924–1934)," *ARCHIVOS de historia del movimiento obrero y la izquierda*, no. 22 (March–August, 2023): 19–39.

117. Caruso and Contreras, "Jerárquicos y sindicalistas," 19–39.

118. Caruso, "La huelga general marítima del Puerto de Buenos Aires," 52 note 114.
119. Martín Albornoz and Diego Galeano, "Anarquistas y policías en el atlántico sudamericano: una red transnacional, 1890–1910," *Boletín del Instituto de Historia Argentina y Americana Dr. Emilio Ravignani*, no. 47 (2017): 101–21.
120. Albornoz and Galeano, "Anarquistas y policías en el atlántico sudamericano."

Chapter 2: The Caribbean Atlantic

1. Antonio Santamaría, "El crecimiento económico de Cuba republicana (1902–1959): Una revisión y nuevas estimaciones en perspectiva comparada (población, inmigración golondrina, ingreso no azucarero y producto nacional bruto)," *Revista de Indias* 60, no. 219, (2000): 527.
2. Santamaría, "El crecimiento económico de Cuba republicana," 530.
3. Antonio Santamaría, *Historia de los ferrocarriles en Cuba, 1830–1995* (Madrid: CSIC, 1992), 32.
4. Consuelo Naranjo Orovio, ed., *Historia de Cuba* (Madrid: Consejo Superior de Investigaciones Científicas, 2009), 437–38.
5. Naranjo Orovio, *Historia de Cuba*, 437–38.
6. "La Empresa Naviera de Cuba y sus vapores," *Cuba Memorias: Historia de Una Isla*, https://cubamemorias.com/la-empresa-naviera-de-cuba-y-sus-vapores-de-pasaje-y-carga.
7. "La Empresa Naviera de Cuba y sus vapores."
8. Luís Prieto-Lavín Coterillo, *Aramos el mar: El último indiano naviero* (Kindle Direct Publishing, 2020), 38.
9. J. Antonio Vidal Rodríguez, "Cadenas migratorias locales, nichos laborales y empresaria les en el colectivo gallego de Cuba: 1899–1959," *Revista Complutense de Historia de América*, no. 32 (2006): 205.
10. Vidal, "Cadenas migratorias," 210.
11. J. Antonio Vidal, *La emigración gallega a Cuba: trayectos migratorios, inserción y movilidad laboral, 1898–1968* (Madrid: CSIC, 2005), 149.
12. Vidal, "Cadenas migratorias," 212.
13. Naranjo Orovio, *Historia de Cuba*, 445; Louis A. Perez, *Cuba: Between Reform and Revolution* (Oxford: Oxford University Press, 2015); Antonio Santamaría, "El crecimiento económico

de Cuba republicana (1902–1959): Una revisión y nuevas estimaciones en perspectiva comparada (población, inmigración golondrina, ingreso no azucarero y producto nacional bruto)," *Revista de Indias*, 60, no. 219 (2000): 197-226; Antonio Santamaría García, *Historia de los ferrocarriles en Cuba, 1830–1995* (Madrid: CSIC, 1992); J. Antonio Vidal Rodríguez, "Cadenas migratorias locales, nichos laborales y empresariales en el colectivo gallego de Cuba: 1899–1959," *Revista Complutense de Historia de América*, 32 (2006): 151; Antonio J. Vidal, *La emigración gallega a Cuba: Trayectos migratorios, inserción y movilidad laboral, 1898–1968* (Madrid: CSIC, 2005).

14. Joan Casanovas Codina, "Movimiento obrero y lucha anticolonial en Cuba después de la abolición de la esclavitud," *Boletín americanista* 45 (1995): 23–41.

15. Joan Casanovas Codina, "La prensa obrera y la evolución ideológico-táctica del obrerismo cubano del siglo XIX," *Signos Históricos*, no. 9 (January–June, 2003), 13–42.

16. David Domínguez-Cabrera, "De aquí la necesidad de un gremio, la necesidad de una tarifa: Conflictos portuarios y derechos laborales en la bahía habanera (1901–1918)," *HiSTOReLo: Revista de Historia Regional y Local* 15, no. 33 (2023), 153–54.

17. "La huelga de Bahía," *La Lucha*, July 1, 1904; "La huelga de Bahía," *La Lucha*, July 9, 1904; Domínguez-Cabrera, "De aquí la necesidad de un gremio," 153–54.

18. Juan Martínez de la Graña, "Desde la Habana," *Germinal*, March 5, 1905.

19. "A los compañeros fogoneros y marineros," *Tierra*, January 13, 1906.

20. *Tierra*, August 19, 1906.

21. Translated from "A los compañeros fogoneros y marineros," *Tierra*, March 17, 1906.

22. "A los compañeros fogoneros y marineros," *Tierra*, March 17, 1906.

23. Bieito Alonso, *Estendendo a rebelión: Sindicalistas marítimos galegos na América Atlántica* (A Coruña: Deputación da Coruña, 2021), 65.

24. Translated from *Cultura Obrera*, May 14, 1912.

25. Translated from "¡Adelante!," *Tierra*, May 8, 1912. The article reproduces a manifesto of the Unión de Fogoneros, Marineros y Similares, signed by the executive committee.

26. Translated from "La huelga de los obreros del puerto," *Tierra*, May 11, 1912.

27. Translated from "A los Trabajadores," *Tierra*, May,18, 1912.
28. "Intensa metamorfosis que se nota en la vida obrera cubana," *Diario de la Marina*, January 1, 1929.
29. Louis A Perez, *Cuba: Between Reform and Revolution* (Oxford: Oxford University Press, 2015), 187.
30. "Sobre ideas y tácticas. Al compañero Juan Martínez de la Graña," *Cultura Obrera* (New York), August 1, 1917.
31. Charles Toth, "Samuel Gompers, el comunismo y la Federación Panamericana del Trabajo," *Revista De Ciencias Sociales* 4 (1973): 481–90.
32. Robert Alexander, *A History of Organized Labor in Cuba* (New York: Bloomsbury Publishing USA, 2002), 26.
33. Translated from Juan Arévalo, "El movimiento obrero en Cuba," *Cosmópolis*, September, 1929.
34. Arévalo, "El movimiento obrero en Cuba."
35. Amparo Sánchez Cobos, *Sembrando ideales: anarquistas españoles en Cuba, 1902–1925* (Seville: CSIC, 2008), 306.
36. Josef Opatrný, "José Antonio Saco y la búsqueda de la identidad cubana," *Ibero-Americana Pragensia* 24 (2010): 229–45.
37. The identification of Arévalo and Cuban reformists with the UGT and with the PSOE (he had an affiliate card of the PSOE section in Havana) was always explicit. Both organizations were considered as the models to follow: "Cuban Federation of Labor follows the UGT tactics in the economic field, and we plan to hold a Congress in a few months and agree on organization of a socialist party, in the style of that of Spain." (Translated from Arévalo, "El movimiento obrero en Cuba.")
38. Arévalo wrote for many publications, including the column "Cuestiones Obreras" in *El País* in 1922 and the column "Patrones y obreros" in *El Heraldo de Cuba*. He was also linked to the weekly *España Nueva*, which he was the administrator of between February 20 and May 13, 1921.
39. Oscar Zanetti and Alejandro Garcia, *Sugar and Railroads: A Cuban History, 1837–1959* (Chapel Hill: University of North Carolina Press, 2017).
40. Juan Arévalo, *Nuestras actividades sindicales en relación con el General Machado y su gobierno* (Havana: Ediciones de Acción Socialista, 1947), 65.
41. Translated from Arévalo, "El movimiento obrero."
42. Arévalo, *Nuestras actividades sindicales*, 69.
43. *A los trabajadores, a los patronos, a las autoridades y a la opinión*

pública en general (pamphlet) (Union de Tripulantes Marítmos de Cuba, 1928).

44. Carleton Beals, *The Crime of Cuba* (Philadelphia: J. P. Lippincott, 1934), 172.

45. Beals, *The Crime of Cuba*, 175.

46. Jorge Domingo Cuadriello, *Diccionario Biobibliográfico de escritores: Españoles en Cuba* Siglo XX (Havana: Editorial Letras Cubanas, 2010), 41.

47. Kirwin Shaffer, "Contesting Internationalists: Transnational Anarchism, Anti-Imperialism and US Expansion in the Caribbean, 1890s–1920s," *EIAL* 22, no 2 (2011): 17.

48. Shaffer, "Contesting Internationalists," 19.

Chapter 3: The North American Atlantic

1. Translated from Genaro Pazos, "De nuestros corresponsales: Mitin monstruo," *Cultura Obrera*, May 14, 1913.

2. Pedro Esteve, "Oh, la patria," *Cultura Obrera*, May 16, 1914.

3. Mónica Álvarez Estévez, "Entre dos orillas: la inmigración gallega en Nueva York: Morriña e identidades transnacionales," *Estudios del Observatorio / Observatorio Studies* 59 (2020): 9; Montse Feu, *Fighting Fascist Spain: Worker Protest from the Printing Press* (Urbana: University of Illinois Press, 2020); Christopher J. Castañeda and Montse Feu, *Writing Revolution: Hispanic Anarchism in the United States* (Urbana: University of Illinois Press, 2019).

4. *Boletín del Consejo Superior de Emigración*, 1916, 168–69.

5. *The Seamen's Bill: Hearings Held before the Committee on the Merchant Marine and Fisheries on House Bill 11372, Thursday, December 14, 1911 [and Monday, January 29, 1912]*, Washington, DC: US Government Printing Office, 1911, 89.

6. Arthur Emil Albrecht, *International Seamen's Union of America: A Study of Its History and Problems* (Washington, DC: US Government Printing Office, 1923), 98.

7. Bieito Alonso Fernández, *Obreiros alén mar: Mariñeiros, fogoneiros e anarquistas galegos en New York (1900–1930)* (Vigo: A Nosa Terra, 2006), 32.

8. P. B. Kennedy and A. S. Link, "The Seamen's Act," *Annals of the American Academy of Political and Social Science* 63 (1916): 232–43.

9. *The Seamen's Bill*, 89.

10. *The Seamen's Bill*; Juan Martínez, "Crónica semanal de los fogoneros," *Cultura Proletaria*, August 20, 1910.
11. Translated from José M. Taracido, "Marinosantiguos," *Fuerza Consciente* (San Francisco), March 7, 1914.
12. Translated from "Nuestra emancipación," *Cultura Proletaria*, June 24, 1911. Dionisio Freijomil Gómez was born in Ferrol on January 6, 1882. He arrived in New York on April 23, 1914, as a sailor on the steamer *Philadelphia* from Southampton. Freijomil was an anarcho-individualist and founder of the libertarian collective Lucifer in New York. He died in Ferrol in January 1922.
13. David M. Struthers, *The World in a City: Multiethnic Radicalism in Early Twentieth–Century Los Angeles* (Urbana: University of Illinois Press, 2019).
14. Hyman Weintraub, *Andrew Furuseth, Emancipator of the Seamen* (Berkeley: University of California Press, 1959), 101–2.
15. Genaro Pazos, "Bosquejo histórico del proletariado español en Norteamérica," *Solidaridad Obrera* (A Coruña), November 15, 1930.
16. Weintraub, *Andrew Furuseth*, 101–2; Struthers, *The World in a City*.
17. Juan Martínez, "De los trabajadores del mar," *Cultura Obrera,* September 27, 1913; "Más allá de las fronteras: El anarquismo argentino en el período de entreguerras" (PhD diss., Universidad Autónoma de Madrid, 2018), 291.
18. "Solidaridad Internacional Obrera," *La Revista Blanca* (Madrid), supplement 120, August 31, *1901*.
19. Kirwin R. Shaffer, "Havana Hub: Cuban Anarchism, Radical Media and the Trans-Caribbean Anarchist Network, 1902–1915," *Caribbean Studies* 37, no. 2 (2009), 45–81, https://www.redalyc.org/articulo.oa?id=39215001002.
20. Jaime Vidal, "Conspirando contra Cultura Proletaria," *Cultura Proletaria*, August 20, 1910.
21. Jon Bekken and Mario Martin Revellado, "Spanish Firemen and Maritime Syndicalism, 1902–1940," in *Writing Revolution: Hispanic Anarchism in the United States*, ed. Christopher J. Castañeda and Montse Feu (Urbana: University of Illinois Press, 2019), 103.
22. William Donald Riddell, "To the Water's Edge of Empire: Domestic Class Struggle, White Merchant Sailors, and the Emerging U.S. Imperial System, 1872–1924" (PhD diss., University of Toronto, 2019), 161.

23. *The Seamen's Bill*, 200; see also, "La Convención de los Obreros del Mar," *Cultura Obrera*, December 9, 1911.

24. Translated from "A los fogoneros de Boston," *Cultura Proletaria*, August 18, 1910.

25. Translated from Juan Martínez, "De los trabajadores del mar," *Cultura Obrera*, September 27, 1913.

26. Juan Zamora Terrés, "El sindicato libre de la marina mercante, un intento de unidad sindical: Notas para una historia del movimiento obrero en la marina mercante" (PhD diss., Universitat Politècnica de Catalunya, 1997), 25.

27. Zamora, *El sindicato libre de la marina mercante*, 34–35.

28. "Craft societies are as necessary as idealistic groups. To abandon the society of trade, not to work actively in it, is to reduce oneself the field of action, to cancel it almost." Translated from Juan Martínez, "Crónica de los fogoneros," *Cultura Obrera*, February 14, 1912.

29. Kirwin Shaffer, *Anarchists of the Caribbean: Countercultural Politics and Transnational Networks in the Age of US Expansion* (Cambridge: Cambridge University Press, 2020), 42.

30. Struthers, *The World in a City*.

31. Jaime Vidal, "Un triunfo moral de los fogoneros," *Cultura Obrera*, November 4, 1911.

32. José Berengher (Berenguer), "De la discusión sale la luz," *Cultura Proletaria*, July 16, 1910.

33. María Migueláñez, "La presencia argentina en la esfera del anarquismo y el sindicalismo internacional," *Historia, Trabajo y Sociedad*, no. 4 (2013): 96.

34. Cole, Struthers, and Zimmer, eds., *Wobblies of the World*, 4.

35. Quoted in Bert Altena, "Analysing Revolutionary Syndicalism. The importance of Community," in *New Perspectives on Anarchism, Labour and Syndicalism: The Individual, the National and the Transnational*, ed. Dave Berry and Constance Bantman (Cambridge: Cambridge Scholars Publishing, 2010), 185.

36. Altena, "Analysing Revolutionary Syndicalism," 187.

37. Van der Linden and Thorpe, *Revolutionary Syndicalism*, 29.

38. J. Naya, "Para lo compañeros de la Unión," *Cultura Obrera*, November 15, 1913.

39. For Sueiro, both Esteve and Malatesta "considered that it was necessary to open up to the workers' movement by participating in collective action and entering the unions, but they did not give up valuing the importance of individual terrorist action or

of small groups, the propaganda of the deed." Susana Sueiro, "Un anarquista en penumbra. Pedro Esteve y la velada red del anarquismo transnacional," *Alcores: Revista de historia contemporánea* 15 (2013): 56.

40. Juan Martínez, "Desde la mar," *Cultura Obrera*, June 21, 1913.
41. "Autonomía y cohesión," *Cultura Obrera*, January 13, 1912.
42. Xan da Graña, "Crónica de Fogoneros," *Cultura Obrera*, January 1, 1912.
43. Translated from Jaime Vidal, "El valor del sindicalismo," *Cultura Obrera*, March 30, 1912.
44. Vidal, "El valor del sindicalismo."
45. Genaro Pazos, "Consideraciones," *Cultura Obrera*, December 9, 1911.
46. Jacy Seixas, "Acerca del militante anarquista: sensibilidad, cultura y ética política, Sao Paulo y Río de Janeiro, 1890–1920," in *Cultura y política del anarquismo en España e Iberoamérica*, ed. Clara E. Lida, and Pablo Yankelevich (Mexico City: El Colegio de México AC, 2012), 311.
47. Translated from "La única vía," *Cultura Obrera*, February 3, 1912.
48. Translated from "La labor en las locales," *Cultura Obrera*, February 24, 1912.
49. Alonso, *Obreiros alén mar*, 94.
50. Although the original minutes of the assemblies are not preserved, part of them were published, as an extract, in the pages of *Cultura Obrera* under the title "Official" in the period between the strikes of 1911 and 1912.
51. Collective aid was also channeled through the assemblies for members who had suffered a serious occupational accident. *Cultura Obrera* reported on a collection of funds by the locals in Galveston, Boston, Norfolk, and Chicago to buy an artificial leg for the sailor Manuel Suárez. See "Cumpliendo encargos," *Cultura Obrera*, November 29, 1913.
52. *Cultura Obrera*, February 3, 1912.
53. Paul Avrich, *The Modern School Movement* (Princeton: Princeton University Press, 1980), 37.
54. Translated from Juan Martínez, "De los trabajadores del mar," *Cultura Obrera,* September 27, 1913.
55. Secundino Brage, "Abajo los tiranos," *Cultura Proletaria*, July 16, 1910.
56. Translated from Lázaro García, "Al pueblo trabajador," *Cultura Obrera*, May 25, 1912.

57. Alonso, *Obreiros alén mar*, 84.

58. Jaime Solá, "Los gallegos en New York," *Vida Gallega* 57 (1914) (Vigo, Spain) .

59. José Ricardo March, *25 historias del Valencia CF que quizá no conozcas* (Valencia: Llibres de la Drassana, 2016), 57.

60. Pietro Di Paola, *The Knights Errant of Anarchy: London and the Italian Anarchist Diaspora, 1880–1917* (Liverpool: Liverpool University Press, 2013).

61. Jorge Uría, "La taberna: Un espacio multifuncional de sociabilidad popular en la Restauración española," *Hispania*, no. 214 (2003): 571–604.

62. Madelon Powers, *Faces along the Bar: Lore and Order in the Workingman's Saloon, 1870–1920* (Chicago: University of Chicago Press, 1999), 66–69.

63. Tom Goyens, *Beer and Revolution: The German Anarchist Movement in New York City, 1880–1914* (Urbana: University of Illinois Press, 2007), 21–22.

64. Translated from Emilio García, "Reflexiones," *Cultura Obrera*, February 23, 1912.

65. Pedro Esteve, "Pro Cultura Obrera," *Cultura Obrera,* February 15, 1912.

66. Translated from *Cultura Obrera*, June 21, 1913.

67. Translated from Sara Hidalgo García de Orellán, "Emocionesentorno a la taberna en España: entre elasco y el orgullo de clase," *Revista Electrónica de Psicología Iztacala* 16, no. 4 (2013): 1324.

68. Esteve, "Pro Cultura Obrera."

69. Juan Martínez, "De los trabajadores del mar," *Cultura Obrera*, June 24, 1911.

70. Translated from *Cultura Obrera*, April 12, 1913.

71. José Filgueira, "Desde Norfolk," *Cultura Proletaria*, August 19, 1911.

72. Juan Martínez, "De los Trabajadores del Mar. Descubriendo verdades," *Cultura Obrera*, December 28, 1912.

73. Translated from José Landeira, "A bordo del "Bordentown," *Cultura Obrera*, January 6, 1912.

74. "La guerra social en Inglaterra," *Cultura Proletaria*, August 19, 1911.

75. *Cultura Proletaria*, June 17, 1911.

76. Jaime Vidal, "Huelga universal de los mares," *Cultura Proletaria*, June 17, 1911.

77. Vidal, "Huelga universal de los mares."

78. "Seamen's Strike at New York," *Press* (Christchurch, New Zealand), June 19, 1911.

79. *Times Dispatch* (Richmond, Va.), June 18, 1911.

80. "Muy importante ¡A los marineros de la Habana!," *Cultura Proletaria*, June 17, 1911.

81. Translated from Juan Martínez, "Movimiento Obrero Marítimo: Crónica de los fogoneros," *Cultura Proletaria*, September 16, 1911.

82. "La Federación Mundial del Transporte," *Cultura Obrera*, February 3, 1912. The first time they called for a universal maritime strike was during the Marine Firemen's strike in the summer of 1911 (*Cultura Proletaria* 61, June 17, 1911).

83. George C. Bodine was an American maritime leader who founded the Atlantic Coast Seamen's Union in New Orleans and later served as vice president of the International Seamen's Union from 1907 to 1910.

84. Jaime Vidal, "Informe sobre la Convención," *Cultura Obrera*, December 23, 1911.

85. Weintraub, *Andrew Furuseth*, 103.

86. Translated from Juan Martínez, "Crónica de los fogoneros," *Cultura Obrera*, March 6, 1912.

87. Bekken and Revellado, *"Spanish Firemen* and Maritime Syndicalism,"* 105.

88. Beken and Revellado, "Spanish Firemen and Maritime Syndicalism," 146; Frederick Sumner Boyd, "The Atlantic Transport Workers Strike," *International Socialist Review*, August 1912: 150–54.

89. Christopher J. Castañeda, "Yours for the Revolution. Cigar Makers, Anarchists, and Brooklyn's Spanish Colony, 1878–1925," in *Hidden Out in the Open: Spanish Migration to the United States (1875–1930)*, ed. Phylis Cancilla Martinelli and Ana Varela-Lago (Louisville: University Press of Colorado, 2019), 159.

90. Beken and Revellado, "Spanish Firemen and Maritime Syndicalism," 147.

91. Alonso, *Estendendo a rebelión*, 95.

92. Arthur Emil Albrecht, *International Seamen's Union of America: A Study of Its History and Problems* (Washington, DC: Bureau of Labor Statistics, 1923), 15–16.

93. M. D. Rodríguez, "A los obreros marítimos," *El Único*, April 12, 1912.

94. José Galán, "Para el "Único" embustero," *Cultura Obrera*, April–May, 1912.
95. Juan Martínez, "De los trabajadores del mar," *Cultura Obrera*, September 27, 1913.
96. Translated from Juan Martínez de la Graña, "De fuera y de casa," *Cultura Obrera*, November 15, 1913.
97. Martínez de la Graña, "De fuera y de casa."
98. Translated from "Para los compañeros de la Unión," *Cultura Obrera*, November 15, 1913.
99. Juan Martínez de la Graña, "Crónica de los fogoneros," *Cultura Obrera*, January 6, 1912.
100. Bekken and Revellado, "Spanish Firemen and Maritime Syndicalism," 108.
101. "La organización industrial de los obreros del transporte," *Cultura Obrera*, April 19, 1913.
102. Bekken and Revellado, "Spanish Firemen and Maritime Syndicalism," 108.
103. Translated from "¿Muertos o vivos?," *Cultura Obrera*, September 18, 1915.
104. Translated from Juan Martínez, "Para los trabajadores del mar," *Cultura Obrera*, October 10, 1914.
105. "If the fellow stokers want the Union, since many say that one must have, let us organize ourselves independently; doing our radical work, it is not useful to pay dues if in the brains of individuals we do not try to instill the principles." Juan Martínez, "Para los fogoneros de Boston," *Cultura Obrera*, June 26, 1915.
106. Translated from "Movimiento de propaganda expropiadora: A todos los anarquistas del mundo," *Regeneración*, May 2, 1914.
107. Translated from "Trabajadores del mar en New York," *Cultura Obrera*, July 4, 1914.
108. H. Gutiérrez, "A los conscientes," *Cultura Obrera*, August 12, 1916; Bieito Alonso, "Migración y sindicalismo: Marineros y anarquistas españoles en Nueva York (1902–1930)," *Historia social*, no. 54 (2006): 129.
109. Bekken and Revellado, "Spanish Firemen and Maritime Syndicalism," 109.
110. Bekken and Revellado, "Spanish Firemen and Maritime Syndicalism," 109–10.
111. Peter Cole, *Wobblies on the Waterfront: Interracial Unionism in Progressive-Era Philadelphia* (Urbana: University of Illinois Press, 2007), 105.

112. Anton Rosenthal, "Radical Border Crossers: The Industrial Workers of the World and Their Press in Latin America," *EIAL* 22, no. 2, (2011): 45.
113. Juan Martínez, "Hay que sacrificarse," *Fuerza Consciente*, February 21, 1914.
114. "La explosión del 'Chancelor' costó la vida a Juan Martínez 'La Graña' ayer," *La Prensa*, August 1, 1928; "Remember," *¡Despertad!*, August 13, 1929.
115. Jennifer Guglielmo, "Transnational Feminism's Radical Past: Lessons from Italian Immigrant Women Anarchists in Industrializing America," *Journal of Women's History* 22, no. 1 (Spring 2010): 15.
116. Pedro Esteve, "Lean y obren en consecuencia," *Cultura Obrera* 109, May 22, 1915.
117. *Regeneración*, November 27, 1915. Among these Spanish anarchists were Román Delgado, Jorge de Borrán (Jesús Iglesias Janeiro), Juan Rodríguez, Ventura Mijón, and Herminio González.
118. *Regeneración*, November 25, 1916.
119. *Cultura Obrera*, November 27, 1911.
120. "La Federación Mundial del Transporte," *Cultura Obrera*, February 3, 1912.
121. Laforcade, "Community Traditions, Labor Insurgencies, and Argentine Shipyard Workers."
122. Pierre Bourdieu, *Lamiseria del mundo* (Buenos Aires: Fondo de Cultura Económica, 1999), 122.
123. James, *Holding Aloft the Banner of Ethiopia*.

Epilogue

1. Michel-Rolph Trouillot, *Silencing the Past: Power and the Production of History* (Boston: Beacon Press, 1995).
2. Sam Davies and Klaus Weinhauer, "Towards a Comparative International History of Dockers," in *Dock Workers: International Explorations in Comparative Labour History, 1790–1970*, ed. Sam Davies, Colin J. Davis, David de Vries, Lex Heerma van Voss, Lidewij Hesselink and Klaus Weinhauer eds. (New York: Routledge: 2000), 24–25.
3. Anton Rosenthal, "Radical Border Crossers: The Industrial Workers of the World and Their Press in Latin America," *EIAL* 22, no. 2, (2011): 47.
4. Rosenthal, "Radical Border Crossers," 48.

5. Kirwin Shaffer, *Anarchists of the Caribbean: Countercultural Politics and Transnational Networks in the Age of US Expansion* (Cambridge: Cambridge University Press, 2020), 110.

6. Kenyon Zimmer, *Immigrants against the State: Yiddish and Italian Anarchism in America* (Urbana: University of Illinois Press, 2013), 4.

7. Martha A. Ackelsberg, *Free Women of Spain: Anarchism and the Struggle for the Emancipation of Women* (Bloomington: Indiana University Press, 1991), 22.

8. Michael Vierhauser, Rick Rabiser, and Paul Grünbacher, "Systems of Systems," in Requirements Monitoring Frameworks: A Systematic Review," *Information and Software Technology*, 2016, https://www.sciencedirect.com/topics/computer-science/systems-of-system

9. Ackelsberg, *Free Women of Spain*, 33–34.

10. Laura Caruso, "Federados, soldados y productores: La militancia sindicalista revolucionaria en el sector marítimo (1910–1924)," *Archivos*, no. 10 (March 2017): 38.

11. Caruso, "Federados, soldados y productores," 40.

Index

La Rebelión (newspaper), 126
Recio, Juan, 124
Rediker, Marcus, 2–3, 10
reformism, 75–79, 82, 104.
  See also Arévalo Vieites,
  Juan
Regeneración (newspaper),
  102
revolutionary syndicalism,
  19–20, 100–101. *See also*
  Unión de Fogoneros,
  Cabos y Engrasadores del
  Atlántico; *specific unions*
Rey, Manuel, 119
Rio de Janeiro, 46–48
Rivas, José, 71
Roca, Rafael, 31
Rodríguez, Andrés, 118
Rodríguez, Manuel D.,
  119–20
Ros, Francisco, 36, 38, 39
Rosenthal, Anton, 132
Rossi, José Gregorio, 44, 53
Roura, José, 59

safety, 49
Sager, Eric, 8
sailing ships, 7, 8, 10–11
sailors: in Argentina, 25, 41,
  60–62; bars in NYC,
  108–09, 111, 113; in
  Chile, 126; as immigrants
  to Argentina, 25; and
  languages, 93; living conditions, 11, 139–40n30;
  newspapers in US, 124;
  racism on ships, 116;
  on steamers vs. sailing
  ships, 7–10; in US, 92,

93, 114, 118, 124. *See also*
  firemen; port workers;
  specific unions
Saint-Imier Congress, 34–35
scabs, 39–40, 57, 125
Schliesen ship, 146–7n106
schools, 37
Seamen's Act (1915), 92
Shaffer, Kirwin, 134
shipping companies: and
  anarchist newspapers,
  106; and bars in NYC,
  112–13; in Cuba, 69–70;
  and FOM, 62–63; and
  government intervention,
  19; hiring police, 118;
  steamership rise and
  losses, 8–9; in US, 93.
  See also strikes
Sobrinos de Herrera, 69,
  70–71, 76. *See also*
  Empresa Naviera de
  Cuba
social democracy, 82
socialism, 31, 33–34, 37,
  143n27. *See also* Abad,
  Gabriel
Socialist Workers' Federation
  congress, 33
Sociedad de Estibadores (Stevedores' Society), 56
Sociedad de Foguistas (Firemen's Society), 61
Sociedad de Herreros,
  Mecánicos, Fundidores
  y Anexos (Society of
  Blacksmiths, Mechanics,
  Smelters, and Ancillary
  Workers), 33, 34

INDEX